JUSTICE HOLMES

The MEASURE of HIS THOUGHT

Only when you have worked alone — when you have felt around you a black gulf of solitude more isolating than that which surrounds the dying man, and in hope and despair have trusted to your own unshaken will, then only will you have achieved. Thus only can you gain the secret isolated joy of the thinker, who knows that a hundred years after he is dead and forgotten, men who never heard of him will be moving to *the measure of his thought* — the subtle rapture of a postponed power, which the world knows not because it has not external trappings, but which to his prophetic vision is more real than that which commands an army.

OLIVER WENDELL HOLMES, JR.,
"The Profession of the Law," conclusion of a lecture delivered to undergraduates
of Harvard University, February 17, 1886. *Speeches* (Boston, 1913), 22–25.

Study of Justice and Mrs. Oliver Wendell Holmes's Washington, D.C. residence,
by Harris & Ewing, 1935.
(*Courtesy of Historical & Special Collections, Harvard Law School Library. Record ID: olvwork392141.
Reproduction from the Library of Congress Prints & Photographs Division*)

JUSTICE HOLMES

The MEASURE of HIS THOUGHT

Anthony
MURRAY

Edwin G.
QUATTLEBAUM III

Clark, New Jersey

Copyright © 2017 by Anthony Murray and Edwin G. Quattlebaum III

ISBN 978-1-61619-388-1

TALBOT PUBLISHING
AN IMPRINT OF
THE LAWBOOK EXCHANGE, LTD.
33 Terminal Avenue
Clark, New Jersey 07066-1321

Please see our website for a selection of our other publications and fine facsimile reprints of classic works of legal history:
www.lawbookexchange.com

COVER: *Upper:* Oliver Wendell Holmes, Jr. Informal full-length portrait of Holmes at the Irish country estate of Leslie and Ethel Scott. 1909. Courtesy of Historical & Special Collections, Harvard Law School Library. Record ID: olvwork389730. *Lower:* Oliver Wendell Holmes, Jr. Informal full-length portrait of Holmes at the Irish country estate of Leslie and Ethel Scott. 1909. Courtesy of Historical & Special Collections, Harvard Law School Library. Record ID: olvwork389731.

Library of Congress Cataloging-in-Publication Data
Names: Murray, Anthony, 1937- | Quattlebaum, Edwin G., 1942- author.
Title: Justice Holmes : the measure of his thought / Anthony Murray, Edwin G. Quattlebaum III.
Description: Clark, NJ : Talbot Publishing, an imprint of The Lawbook Exchange, Ltd., 2017. | Includes bibliographical references and index.
Identifiers: LCCN 2017037086 | ISBN 9781616193881 (hardcover : alk. paper)
Subjects: LCSH: Holmes, Oliver Wendell, Jr., 1841-1935. | Law--Language. | Law--Methodology. | Law--United States.
Classification: LCC KF8745.H6 .M877 2017 | DDC 347.73/2634--dc23
LC record available at https://lccn.loc.gov/2017037086

Printed in the United States of America on acid-free paper

To Kathleen and Ruth

Table of Contents

Foreword   ix

1   Introduction   1
2   Beverly Farms   5
3   Laboratory for a Thinker   19
4   Civil War   37
5   Defining Law   51
6   Erudition   71
7   Style of Holmes's Opinions   83
8   Massachusetts Supreme Judicial Court   89
9   United States Supreme Court   95
10   The Lochner Era and Judicial Restraint   101
11   Speech   115
12   Conclusion   169

Acknowledgments   173
Bibliography   175
Index   183

Foreword

"The most illustrious figure in the history of American law"

OLIVER WENDELL HOLMES, JR. is best known for his lengthy and distinguished judicial career. Legal scholars, judges, lawyers, historians, and colleagues recognize Holmes as the greatest judicial figure in American history. Most prominently, he was a thinker. The range and originality of his thought were remarkable and probably unexcelled by any American judge. Tributes to Holmes and his gift of thought and expression abound.

A distinguished federal judge, Charles E. Wyzanski, Jr., said about Holmes:

> [L]ike the Winged Victory of Samothrace he is the summit of hundreds of years of civilization, the inspiration of years to come. ...[1]

Judge Richard A. Posner of the U. S. Court of Appeals for the Seventh Circuit, who has made a life's study of Holmes, described him as "the most illustrious figure in the history of American law."[2]

---

[1] Charles E. Wyzanski, Jr., *Whereas: A Judge's Premises* (Boston, 1944), 43–44; *see also*, Wyzanski, "The Democracy of Justice Oliver Wendell Holmes," *Vanderbilt Law Review* 7 (1954): 311, 323.

[2] Richard A. Posner (ed.), *The Essential Holmes: Selections from the Letters, Speeches, Judicial Opinions, and Other Writings of Oliver Wendell Holmes, Jr.* (Chicago, 1992), iv.

Anthony Lewis, the acclaimed journalist and First Amendment scholar, said, "Holmes was the closest we have to a poet judge."[3]

Former Secretary of State Dean Acheson said:

> One of the slipperiest words I know is "great." But I think the greatest man I have known, that is, the essence of man living, man thinking, man baring himself to the lonely emptiness — or the reverse — of the universe, was Holmes. Brandeis was eminent, but not his equal.[4]

The prominent historian and scholar James MacGregor Burns wrote that when Holmes was appointed to the Supreme Court in 1902:

> He was an accomplished lawyer and judge — chief justice of the Massachusetts Supreme Judicial Court — but also a scholar, the author of *The Common Law*, a pioneering study of the formation of law. Even more, Holmes was a kind of Enlightenment philosopher, son of an eminent man of letters, acquainted with such literati as Emerson and Longfellow, one of the few Americans who could converse on easy terms in London with John Stuart Mill and Prime Minister William Gladstone.[5]

---

[3] Anthony Lewis, *Freedom for the Thought that We Hate: A Biography of the First Amendment* (New York, 2007), 33.
[4] David C. Acheson, et alia, *Among Friends: Personal Letters of Dean Acheson* (New York, 1980), May 24, 1960, 182–183.
[5] James MacGregor Burns, *Packing the Court: The Rise of Judicial Power and the Coming Crisis of the Supreme Court* (New York, 2009), 116.

Of Holmes, the American poet Archibald MacLeish, said,

> [Holmes] was a man of the world who was also a philosopher, who was incidentally a lawyer. The result was that he was a very great judge."[6]

Isaiah Berlin commented, "The German poet Heine, in one of his writings told us not to underestimate the quiet philosopher sitting in his study ..."[7]

And finally, Roscoe Pound, Dean of Harvard Law School, said, "The world now moved to the measure of Holmes's thought." [8]

We now explore the reasons for this high praise.

---

[6] Archibald MacLeish and E.F. Pritchard, Jr. (eds.), "Introduction," in *Law and Politics: Occasional Papers of Felix Frankfurter, 1913-1938* (New York, 1939), xvii. *See* Alpheus Thomas Mason, *Harlan Fiske Stone: Pillar of the Law* (New York, 1956), 774.

[7] "A Message to the 21st Century," in *New York Review of Books*, October 23, 2014.

[8] *Harvard Law Review* 35 (1921): 449.

Oliver Wendell Holmes, Jr.'s funeral. From the left: PMG James Farley, Mrs. Roosevelt, President Roosevelt, and the White House military attaché, Col. E.M. Watson.
(*Courtesy of Library of Congress*)

1

INTRODUCTION

ON MARCH 8, 1933, Oliver Wendell Holmes, Jr. welcomed to his home at 1720 Eye Street in Washington, D.C., an unusual guest. Four days after taking the oath of office to begin his first term as President of the United States, Franklin Delano Roosevelt paid a visit to Holmes, who had retired after serving for thirty years as Justice of the United States Supreme Court. The occasion was to celebrate Holmes's 92nd birthday. Also present were Roosevelt's wife Eleanor, his son James, Felix Frankfurter, who had arranged the meeting, and Holmes's law secretary Donald Hiss. The President's visit was a fitting tribute to a great American.[1]

Fascination with this particular Supreme Court justice seems endless. He inspired a hit Broadway play and a best-selling novel.[2] A mountain in Alaska was named after him. He

---

[1] Katie Louchheim (ed.), *The Making of the New Deal: The Insiders Speak* (Cambridge, Massachusetts, 1983), 36–38; Felix Frankfurter, *Felix Frankfurter Reminisces* (Harlan Phillips, ed., 1962), 241–242; G. Edward White, *Justice Oliver Wendell Holmes: Law and the Inner Self* (New York, 1993), 469–470.

[2] Catherine Drinker Bowen, *Yankee from Olympus: Justice Holmes and His Family* (Boston, 1944). The Broadway play *The Magnificent Yankee* (1946) became a movie in 1950.

was on a postage stamp. His birthdays were celebrated on the front pages of *The New York Times*.[3] Among U. S. Supreme Court justices, only John Marshall, and perhaps Louis D. Brandeis, come close to attracting as much interest — both lay and professional — over 227 years. "The automobile industry has Henry Ford," summarized one writer; "jazz, Louis Armstrong; Hollywood, Marilyn Monroe; and baseball, Babe Ruth. American law has Oliver Wendell Holmes."[4]

Biographies abound. Some openly fawn, others show a revisionist impulse to "balance," even scandalize. Francis Biddle's is one of the best first-hand accounts. Mark DeWolfe Howe's is the only authorized biography, with earliest access to the massive trove of Holmes family sources, and arguably the most reliable. But some biographers appear to feed upon Justice Holmes's detractors, emphasizing claims that he was arrogant, a cold intellectual, judicially inconsistent, even fascist. They are wrong, as we demonstrate.

Holmes spent nearly all his days either on Beacon Hill in Boston, or within blocks of the Supreme Court in Washington, D.C. or at his summer home at Beverly Farms. A few biographers follow Holmes to England, Ireland, and the continent — including one rigorous climb of the Swiss Alps. Such details about Holmes have long been available. They are not discussed in our book. Instead, we analyze a subtler, more-monumental form of Holmes's humanity: Holmes the thinker. Twenty-first century readers, especially those tempted to

---

[3] Albert W. Alschuler, *Law Without Values: The Life, Work, and Legacy of Justice Holmes* (Chicago, 2000), 15; Liva Baker, *The Justice from Beacon Hill: The Life and Times of Oliver Wendell Holmes* (New York, 1991), 8.
[4] Quoted in Alschuler, *Law Without Values*, 15.

conclude that Americans have little respect for art or ideas, are reminded in this book that the country can produce a thinker who practiced a kind of love affair with language.

How was this young mind formed? How did the Civil War affect it? What was the impact of a nearly monastic decade, practicing law and studying the deepest historical roots of our law — ultimately bearing fruit in his famous Lowell Lectures and his book that most lawyers have at least heard of, *The Common Law*? We will see the astounding breadth and depth of his reading, of his eloquent and prolific correspondence.

We include a description of Holmes's letters, often written at Beverly Farms, a few miles north of Boston. Beverly Farms was the place where Holmes spent nearly half a century of summers, where he could relax, read, and write. It was the place that served to stimulate the ideas that often became the embodiment of his thought.

This volume proves especially timely in the wake of the death of former Supreme Court Justice Antonin Scalia. It contrasts Justice Scalia's opinions with Justice Holmes's open-minded refusal to inject his own views into his decisions, and with the gentlemanly style of his opinions. These qualities form a part of "The Measure of His Thought," the subtitle of the book.

Justice Holmes's landmark dissents, among his countless other opinions, have made an enduring contribution to this nation, to which he willed his modest estate when he died at nearly 94 years of age. "I like to pay taxes," Holmes said. "With them I buy civilization."[5]

---

[5] Felix Frankfurter, *Mr. Justice Holmes and the Supreme Court* Rev. Ed. (Cambridge, Massachusetts, 1961), 71.

Oliver Wendell Holmes, Jr., at Beverly Farms circa 1880. Unidentified woman on porch.
(*Courtesy of Historical & Special Collections, Harvard Law School Library. Record ID: olvwork389587*)

2

BEVERLY FARMS

"Oh, that house!"

WE VISITED BEVERLY FARMS with John Palfrey, the great-grandson of John Gorham Palfrey, Holmes's friend and executor of his estate. John Palfrey is the current Head of School, Phillips Academy, Andover. Coincidentally, Andover was where Dr. Holmes, the father of Justice Holmes, was a schoolboy who graduated in 1825, later wrote an 1878 Andover centennial tribute poem "The School-Boy" which became nationally famous, and where the school's Oliver Wendell Holmes Library was named in his honor. Andover's head John Palfrey was the former Henry N. Ess III Professor of Law at Harvard Law School, and John Gorham Palfrey's family donated to Harvard University a huge collection of Holmes objects, papers, and photographs. When John Palfrey helped navigate us to Beverly Farms, all three of us sensed that, of all the properties where Justice Holmes lived — regular as well as summer residences — the Hale Street house is one of two standing, in something close to what he would recognize, and that something big for America happened right here on Hale Street.

The rest have disappeared. As one Boston historian wrote, "Ironically, none of Dr. Holmes's Boston residences remains

Oliver Wendell Holmes Library (Phillips Academy, Andover, Massachusetts) was built in 1929 and is named for Oliver Wendell Holmes, Sr. Charles A. Platt, Architect, Gottscho-Schleisner, Inc., photographer. June 5, 1937.
(*Courtesy of Library of Congress*)

intact in spite of his fame in the city, the U.S., and Britain."[1] On March 8, 1841, little OWH Jr. was born to Beacon Hill at 8 Montgomery Place. He and his family continued to live there until 1857.[2] That year, as a 16-year-old freshman, Wendell Holmes left home to board at a Harvard College rooming house on Linden Street near the Yard.[3] The same year, his parents made 21 Charles Street (later renumbered 164 Charles Street) the family residence until 1870, when they

---

[1] Mary Melvin Petronella (ed.), *Victorian Boston Today: Twelve Walking Tours* (Boston, 2004), 125.
[2] Mark DeWolfe Howe, *Justice Oliver Wendell Holmes*, vol. I, *The Shaping Years: 1841–1870* (Cambridge, Massachusetts, 1957), 2.
[3] *Ibid.*, 39.

moved a few blocks around the corner to 296 Beacon Street.[4] After his two years across the river at Harvard, and his nearly three years in the Civil War, Wendell returned home to his mother and father at 21 Charles and 296 Beacon. He and his bride — his schoolteacher's daughter Fanny Dixwell — continued to live with Dr. and Mrs. Holmes after their June 17, 1872 wedding. In 1875, the young couple rented rooms above a drugstore at 10 Beacon Street.[5] By 1883 Fanny had found a little house which they could call their own, just around the corner at 9 Chestnut Street,[6] a short walk to the courthouse for Holmes, who was now a Justice on the Massachusetts Supreme Judicial Court. In 1889, after his mother's and sister's deaths, Wendell and Fanny gave up their 9 Chestnut house (which still exists but in remodeled form) to move down Beacon Hill a few blocks, and look after the widowed Dr. Holmes at 296 Beacon Street. There they stayed even after Dr. Holmes's death in 1894.

Finally, in 1902, when Holmes was appointed as a United States Supreme Court Justice, he and Fanny left Beacon Hill for good. After a few months in a friend's house at 10 Lafayette Square,[7] Holmes bought a 4-story brick home at 1720 Eye Street in 1903, one block west and two blocks north

---

[4] Petronella (ed.), *Victorian Boston Today*, 124–125, 240n.
[5] John S. Monagan, *The Grand Panjandrum: Mellow Years of Justice Holmes* (Lanham, Maryland, 1988), 32.
[6] *Ibid.*, Monagan referred to it as 9 "Orchard" Street and then 9 "Chestnut" Street.
[7] Baker, *The Justice from Beacon Hill*, 372.

of the White House.[8] There he remained through Fanny's death in 1929 and until his own death in 1935.

These were all winter residences. Before Beverly Farms, young Holmes had brief stints at two previous summer homes. Between 1849 and 1855, Dr. Holmes owned woodsy acreage on remnants of a Wendell family estate, "Canoe Meadow," just south of Pittsfield on the Housatanic River. As the 5'1" boy entered his teens, Wendell fished for pickerel, rowed, swam, shot, walked through the woods, but kept reading and studying his Latin and French when he wasn't outdoors. Not far away in the Berkshires were other summer residents or frequent visitors, many of them famous authors. But after seven summers of nearly 5 months each, maintaining the property became too expensive for Dr. Holmes. In 1856 he had to sell it, lamenting its loss for the rest of his life. The only trace today is a "Holmes Road" in the area.[9]

In October 1873, a little over a year after their wedding, Wendell and Fanny purchased a farm at Mattapoisett on Buzzards Bay, near a vacation home of Holmes's senior law partner and mentor George Shattuck. At first the Holmeses owned one-half of the house there, a caretaker owning the other half, but Holmes bought him out in 1883. Friends like William James and Owen Wister visited during the annual three weeks the young Holmeses tried to spend in Mattapoisett for fourteen summers. In the spring of 1888, a brush-fire burned the house to the ground.[10] Bereft of a vacation place, in May and June 1888

---

[8] Monagan, *The Grand Panjandrum*, 36.
[9] Baker, *The Justice from Beacon Hill*, 54–56.
[10] Howe, *Justice Oliver Wendell Holmes*, I, *The Shaping Years*, 249, 261–262, 276; II, *The Proving Years: 1870–1882* (Cambridge, Massachusetts, 1963), 10, 23–24, 253.

Wendell and Fanny travelled by train — "9,000 miles in one car!" — to Chicago and on to San Diego and up the Pacific coast to Washington state and British Columbia. They returned by June 8 and shortly thereafter they left again, for two months at Niagara Falls. But first, they checked on the widowed Dr. Holmes at Beverly Farms, where he and his wife had been summering since some time after 1877 when daughter Amelia's husband John Turner Sargent died leaving her property there.[11] Summer 1889 was the first time that Wendell and Fanny began steadily vacationing in Beverly Farms. Justice Holmes's final summer there, just months before his death, was 1934. No record — of which we are aware — verifies the following bold claim: It appears that Wendell enjoyed the house on Hale Street for 46 years — although the first few of those years may have been spent at his parents' other Beverly Farms house nearby.

For a complete residential inventory: The two previous Holmes summer homes, in the Berkshires and at Buzzards Bay; and all of Wendell's Beacon Hill residences, from 8 Montgomery Place at birth (later renamed Bosworth Street and torn down for commercial expansion),[12] to 21 Charles Street (later renumbered 164 Charles but now a parking lot), to the rented rooms above the drugstore (now a pizza restaurant) at

---

[11] Baker, *The Justice from Beacon Hill*, 293–294; White, *Justice Oliver Wendell Holmes*, 225.
[12] Howe, *Justice Oliver Wendell Holmes*, I, *The Shaping Years*, 2.

Justice and Mrs. Oliver Wendell Holmes's summer residence, Beverly Farms, Massachusetts, 1928. (*Courtesy of Historical & Special Collections, Harvard Law School Library. Record ID: olvwork392160*)

10 Beacon Street next door to the famous Boston Athenaeum, to Fanny's and Wendell's first little house of their own at 9 Chestnut (still standing but in modernized form), to their final Beacon Hill residence at 296 Beacon Street (replaced by what was recently a dilapidated residence with an unfinished plywood front and several unclaimed newspapers collecting on the top stoop), to their 4-story brick home at 1720 Eye Street in Washington (now a stone-fronted bank);[13] — only one of the eight residences has survived in roughly the same form. Other than the Hale Street house in Beverly Farms, the only traces are a Holmes Road south of Pittsfield, a renovated version of the little home at 9 Chestnut, and the house next door to 296 Beacon Street where some of Dr. Holmes's books were stored.[14]

---

[13] Erwin N. Griswold, "Foreword," in Sheldon M. Novick (ed.), *The Collected Works of Justice Holmes: Complete Public Writings and Selected Judicial Opinions of Oliver Wendell Holmes* (Chicago, 1995), xv.

[14] Petronella (ed.), *Victorian Boston Today*, 240n.

Beverly Farms today.
(*Courtesy of the authors*)

A city like Boston experiences more bulldozing than a North Shore town like Beverly Farms.

The house on Hale Street, rented in part or in full until Justice Holmes finally purchased the whole place to avoid getting evicted in 1909,[15] today stands pretty much intact, virtually alone (except for 6 short years, 1883–1889, at their little 9 Chestnut Street home on Beacon Hill) as the only residence where you can walk around it and through it. To do so is to re-live Holmes's daily routine — 46 years of meals and bedtimes; of hours studying petitions for writs of certiorari (which Holmes nicknamed "petes for certs") sent from Washington by a Supreme Court clerk;[16] of pondering upcoming opinions, sometimes after a nearby lunch with legal friends, as happened a few weeks before the epic 1919 *Abrams v. U.S.* ruling; of writing remarkable letters; of taking

---

[15] Monagan, *The Grand Panjandrum*, 114.
[16] *Ibid.*

walks to kibbitz with the railroad crossing guard and postmaster;[17] of daily drives in the woods or along the North Shore; of Holmes's joining the bicycle craze in 1895, sometimes riding 15 or 20 miles in a day;[18] of the lighter reading, often Fanny reciting aloud while the Justice played a form of solitaire called "Canfield;"[19] of receiving reporters — relaxed in his sack coat and moccasins — or famous guests; of taking tea with ladies in the Beverly Farms neighborhood.[20]

A September 6, 1925, letter from Justice Holmes to John C.H. Wu, a young legal acolyte in China whom he had invited to Beverly Farms, showed how much he loved those drives along the North Shore:

> [F]or two hours I drive and motor about this beautiful and interesting region, which I am sorry that you did not see. One may gaze over lonely cliffs upon the seas or pass along smooth boulevards by crowded beaches, or skirt windswept downs and fine inland farms, or evoke the past by visiting houses built two centuries and a half ago. That is not long for China but it is long enough for romance.[21]

---

[17] *Ibid*, 34–36.
[18] Baker, *The Justice from Beacon Hill*, 311–312; Monagan, *The Grand Panjandrum*, 108.
[19] Monagan, *The Grand Panjandrum*, 50.
[20] *Ibid.*, 65–66.
[21] Justice Oliver Wendell Holmes to John C.H. Wu, Sept. 6, 1925, in "Some Unpublished Letters of Justice Holmes" (Reprinted from *T'ien Hsia Monthly*, December, 1935), p. 280. Oliver Wendell Holmes, Jr., Addenda, 1818–1978, Box 4, Folder 7. Courtesy of Historical & Special Collections, Harvard Law School Library. Available online at http://nrs.harvard.edu/urn-3:HLS.Libr:8670632?n=17.

As you walk up the same driveway that Holmes walked, and browse through the same barn in the back, and enter the house's front door, and notice the same fireplace, and the same elevator-well installed near the end of his life just before moving his bed downstairs, and learn about a wrap-around veranda partially replaced by a lovely expanded living room, and look out the upstairs window toward the sea, you realize that this house assisted as a muse, for hundreds of stunningly eloquent letters — written and received — for arguably the most famous judge and legal mind in U.S. history.

In front of this fireplace, Justice Holmes doubtless worked on writs of certiorari, read, and wrote letters. The authors received unprecedented access to the indoors of this Beverly Farms summer home — the only surviving structure directly and personally associated with the life of Justice Holmes.
(*Courtesy of the authors*)

The barn in the back, by the way, was where the Justice probably stored his bicycle from 1895 on. This barn may also have been where the Holmes family kept its horses & buggy, for daily drives along the seashore or into the woods, and where one midnight the headstrong Fanny, refusing to wait until morning, commandeered a driver and two horses to ride 35 miles through the night, arriving at 1:30 a.m. in Boston, to check on Holmes's return from England.[22] Unlike fancier summer compounds not far away, at toney addresses like "Manchester-by-the-Sea," Holmes proudly referred to the Hale Street house as his "box," at "Beverly-by-the-Depot." The wooden frame house, writes biographer John Monagan, was "undistinguishable and the decor unremarkable, but it was comfortable and commodious." Its most noteworthy article of adornment was a wood carving made by Fanny, true to her Bowditch family maritime tradition.[23]

In later years, Fanny tended to keep the bamboo screens down and the shades drawn. After her rheumatism and other illnesses, Fanny developed a sensitivity to light and kept certain areas of their houses dark. Isabella Wigglesworth, the wife of Fanny's nephew, has described the house at Beverly Farms:

> Oh that house! I wish you could have seen it then. Not one ray of light penetrated it. Everything was hermetically sealed. There was a porch with rattan curtains that were rolled down to the floor and shades drawn in the windows of the house and electric lights going all the time. [24]

---

[22] Monagan, *The Grand Panjandrum*, 74–75.
[23] Ibid., 34–36.
[24] Ibid., 54.

Oliver Wendell Holmes, Jr. and Beverly farms crossing-tender.
September, 1928. Arthur E. Sutherland, photographer.
(*Courtesy of Historical & Special Collections, Harvard Law School Library.
Record ID: olvwork390426*)

Holmes shared his love of literature with the Beverly Farms crossing-tender. He loaned him a copy of *Moby Dick*, saying that, according to his secretary Arthur E. Sutherland, "in it was the mystery and terror of the universe." Sutherland and Holmes walked around the square daily and stopped to exchange opinions with the watchman.[25] Incidentally, between 1849 and 1856 *Moby Dick*'s author, Herman Melville, had been a neighbor and patient of Dr. Holmes out in the Berkshires, and in fact Melville's address there was 780 Holmes Road, named for the Doctor.[26]

Holmes spent hours on the second floor, in his study, reading. He supplemented his own library with books from the Boston Athenaeum and the local Beverly Farms library. He liked to depart from his usual diet of serious reading with a mystery or a French novel.[27]

This 8-bedroom house was Holmes's escape from Beacon Hill, from the state's Supreme Judicial Court, later from his 1720 Eye Street residence in a sweltering Washington before air-conditioning, and from the old Supreme Court of the United States located down in the basement of the Capitol.

Today, drifting from room to room, or walking outside around the house, or rummaging through the old barn in back, you can sense, at the Hale Street house, Holmes's transcendent power. The intensity with which he always read, researched, studied, and wrote, in his Boston and Washington workplaces, needed a counterpoise of relaxation, where he could finally wear what he called a "soft shirt" and collar.[28] Beverly Farms was it. Here, his correspondence with friends from afar flourished, perhaps more than anywhere else given

---

[25] Inscription on photograph, "Oliver Wendell Holmes, Jr. and Beverly Farms crossing-tender," Arthur E. Sutherland, photographer. Harvard Law School Library. Record ID: olvwork390426.
[26] Petronella (ed.), *Victorian Boston Today*, 237n.
[27] Monagan, *The Grand Panjandrum*, 34–36.
[28] Baker, *The Justice from Beacon Hill*, 15, 306.

its more relaxed routine. It would not be much of a stretch to say that books, some 14,000 of them in various residences, and ideas, were his closest friends — indeed a kind of substitute family — with which he physically shared these very rooms. One of his secretaries, Thomas Corcoran, claimed that the "family Bible" (Holmes's legendary "black book") listed 3,475 titles.[29] Holmes's prolific erudition, scholarship, judicial opinions, and brilliant correspondence represented his kind of intimacy — for people not in the same room.

Beverly Farms was Holmesian intimacy: once removed. In 1913 the house acquired a white kitten, whom the Justice called a "tyrant." Notable guests on his veranda or upstairs guestrooms included Senator and Mrs. Albert J. Beveridge, the Louis Brandeises, the Frederick Pollocks, the Felix Frankfurters, Harold Laski, lawyers for Sacco & Vanzetti, reporters covering rumors that President Theodore Roosevelt had nominated Holmes to the United States Supreme Court, and the Justice's secretaries like Thomas Corcoran, Francis Biddle, Harvey Bundy, and Alger Hiss.[30] One Beverly Farms friend, Timmy O'Brien, brought his accordion and amused the Justice with Irish songs.[31] If Holmes was asleep when a lady guest arrived, Fanny would take a cane out of the umbrella rack and poke the ceiling to wake him up.[32] But as you walk through it, the Beverly Farms house feels more like a house for ideas, instead of a house for colorful guests or for children.

---

[29] Monagan, *The Grand Panjandrum*, 105.
[30] *Ibid.*, 22–24, 118–120.
[31] *Ibid.*, 109.
[32] *Ibid.*, 65–66.

Holmes family, 1860. Left to right: Edward Holmes, brother (standing); Mrs. Amelia Lee Jackson Holmes, mother; Amelia Holmes, sister (standing); Oliver Wendell Holmes, Jr.; Dr. Oliver Wendell Holmes, Sr.
(*Courtesy of Historical & Special Collections, Harvard Law School Library.*
Record ID: olvwork389553)

3

Laboratory for a Thinker

"The education of a child begins 250 years before birth."

How did such a mind develop? What was the recipe for the kind of excellence Holmes developed over his lifetime? Historian James MacGregor Burns's comment, noted earlier, connecting the younger Holmes to the intellectual power of John Stuart Mill, is appropriate.

Mill was born in 1806, just 35 years before Justice Holmes. Mill's father James Mill, with the help of the philosopher Jeremy Bentham, programmed virtually every aspect of young John's schooling. Historians of philosophy have described James Mill's remarkable "laboratory" for raising his son John Stuart Mill.

> The younger Mill was seen as the crown prince of the Philosophic Radical movement and his famous education reflected the hopes of his father and Bentham. Under the dominating gaze of his father, he was taught Greek beginning at age three and Latin at eight. He read histories, many of the Greek and Roman classics, and Newton by eleven. He studied logic and math, moving to political economy and legal philosophy in his early teens, and then went on to metaphysics. His training facilitated active command of the material through the requirement that he

teach his younger siblings and through evening walks with his father when the precocious pupil would have to tell his father what he learned that day. His year in France in 1820 led to fluency in French and initiated his lifelong interest in French thought and politics. As he matured, his father and Bentham both employed him as an editor. In addition, he founded a number of intellectual societies and study groups and began to contribute to periodicals, including the *Westminster Review*.[1]

Oliver Wendell Holmes, Jr., did not quite experience this degree of calculated child rearing. But he benefited from a different kind of "laboratory." Consider its ingredients: family, locality, schools, books, and friends. This combination of circumstances produced arguably the greatest justice of the Supreme Court this country has ever seen — and one of its greatest thinkers. It is worth taking a closer look at these ingredients.

Justice Holmes once said that the education of a child begins 250 years before birth.[2] Maybe he had in mind his own

---

[1] *Internet Encyclopedia of Philosophy: A Peer-Reviewed Academic Source*, "John Stuart Mill (1806–1873)," Biography section, http://www.iep.utm.edu/milljs/. Nearly three centuries earlier, French Renaissance philosopher Michel de Montaigne's education likewise began in early childhood and followed a pedagogical plan that his father had developed. See Tim Parks, "Montaigne: What Was Truly Courageous?" *New York Review of Books*, November 24, 2016, Vol. LXII Number 18, p. 59: "Montaigne," writes Parks, "was the product of an educational experiment at a time when those who could afford such things had become fascinated by the possibilities of social and psychological engineering."

[2] Edward J. Bander (ed.), *Justice Holmes Ex Cathedra* (Buffalo, 1991), 251.

family — Olivers, Wendells, Holmeses. All three branches arrived in New England as early as 1632 through the 1650's. It is said that Holmes's family lineage goes back to a 17th-century barrister in London. Relatives included Anne Bradstreet, various Cabots,[3] Dorothy Quincy, soldiers in the American Revolution, judges. Young Wendell's grandfathers were Abiel Holmes and Charles Jackson. Wendell's father was Oliver Wendell Holmes, Sr.[4] Years later, Justice Holmes told President Franklin D. Roosevelt, "I remember my father's story of his father bringing home for lunch a friend he had met downtown in Boston that day and the friend said 'I saw that little West Indian Bastard this morning,' meaning Alexander Hamilton."[5]

Grandfather Abiel Holmes was an orthodox Calvinist minister. He contributed a stubborn puritanical streak which neither Oliver Wendell Holmes, Sr. nor Oliver Wendell Holmes, Jr. could entirely shed, despite themselves.[6]

Abiel was also a writer — of biographies, history, poetry. His writings demonstrated intellectual curiosity tinged with skepticism for conventional wisdom, which he passed on to his son and grandson. Son recalled that Abiel's "highest

---

[3] Baker, *The Justice from Beacon Hill*, 39–40.
[4] Autobiographical sketch for college album, by Oliver Wendell Holmes, Jr., July 2, 1861, quoted in Frederick C. Fiechter, Jr., "The Preparation of an American Aristocrat," *New England Quarterly* 6(1933): 3–5.
[5] Monagan, *The Grand Panjandrum*, 2.
[6] Howe, *Holmes-Laski Letters*, II, 1278; Howe, *Justice Oliver Wendell Holmes*, I, *The Shaping Years*, 20–21, 252n, 284; vol. II, *The Proving Years: 1870–1882*, 282; White, *Justice Oliver Wendell Holmes*, 23, 496n; Baker, *The Justice from Beacon Hill*, 28–29.

literary pleasure" in writing volumes of history was to "verify a doubtful legend" or to "disprove a questionable tradition" — in short, "to get at the absolute fact" of history.[7]

Wendell's maternal grandfather was Judge Charles Jackson, who rose from a respected textile investor and lawyer — "He will prove himself the American Blackstone" said one legal mentor — to a justice of the Massachusetts Supreme Judicial Court.[8] Wendell's wife Fanny was convinced that Judge Jackson's career and character inspired Wendell toward law and jurisprudence for what he considered — like a Boston Puritan — his calling.[9]

Judge Jackson's example no doubt made a deep impression on Wendell, but he was not the only jurist in Justice Holmes's heritage. A generation earlier, great-grandfather Oliver Wendell, who worked with John and Sam Adams during the Revolution, had later served as a judge of the Suffolk County probate court.[10]

Young Wendell's father, Dr. Oliver Wendell Holmes, was the most influential figure in his early life. Father did not micromanage son's life as James Mill did John Stuart Mill's, but even late in his life son referred to father as "my governor." Some scholars have mistaken Junior's occasional aggravation for outright hostility toward Senior. But there

---

[7] White, *Justice Oliver Wendell Holmes*, 18–19.
[8] Baker, *The Justice from Beacon Hill*, 39–40.
[9] Howe, *Justice Oliver Wendell Holmes*, I, *The Shaping Years*, 178n.
[10] Baker, *The Justice from Beacon Hill*, 31.

Oliver Wendell Holmes, c. 1879. Oct. 14. Photograph by Armstrong & Co.
(*Courtesy of Library of Congress*)

was plenty of affinity and love, as well as son's impatience for following his own path.

Growing up in the household of a Calvinist minister, Holmes the elder rejected his father Abiel's calling, as Wendell would his father's. But skepticism of religious orthodoxy — and of everything else — within both Holmes Sr. and Jr. had begun. "If to question everything be unlawful and dangerous," Sr. once said, "we had better undeclare our independence at once; for what the Declaration means is the right to question everything, even the truth of its own fundamental proposition."[11]

As a schoolboy at Phillips Academy, Andover in the 1820's, Holmes Sr. was already on his way to "question everything," as would his son the legal scholar and judge. A history of Andover described a memorable incident in Holmes Sr.'s time as a student there:

> The most famous disciplinary case ... was the beating that Oliver Wendell Holmes received at the hands of [assistant headmaster] Jonathan Clement ... A fellow student remembers Holmes's stoicism: "What a noble boy he was! Clement would have stopped if he had only said he was sorry, but he wouldn't say it. There he stood, and let him welt him. He never flinched nor cried. ..."[12]

After Andover, Harvard College, and a few miserable months at Harvard Law School, Holmes Sr. turned from Harvard Law School to Harvard Medical School for two years, and an extra year studying with a pathologist in Paris. He wrote his parents, "I have more fully learned three principles since I have been in Paris: not to take authority when I have no facts; not to guess when I can know; not to think a man must take physic because he is sick."[13] Holmes Jr. absorbed two of these same principles for himself.

---

[11] Howe, *Justice Oliver Wendell Holmes*, I, *The Shaping Years*, 17.
[12] Frederick S. Allis, Jr., *Youth from Every Quarter: A Bicentennial History of Phillips Academy, Andover* (Hanover, New Hampshire, 1979), 159.
[13] Holmes, Sr., to Abiel and Sarah Holmes, Aug. 13, 1833, in John T. Morse, Jr., *Life and Letters of Oliver Wendell Holmes* (Boston, 1896), I, 107.

Holmes Sr. did not feel comfortable, though, as a practicing physician. "Giving this up" — as his son recalled in 1861, no doubt with a competitive son's minimizing edge — his father had "since supported himself by acting as a professor [and later dean at age 38] of the Medical School of Harvard College, by lecturing and by writing a number of books."[14] Jr. too would be a professor at Harvard College, then at Harvard Law School, as well as serving on the Board of Overseers. Jr. would deliver the Lowell Lectures like his father, and both would prove to be sought-after speakers.

Once, in July 1880 at Harvard's Memorial Hall, Sr. and Jr. lectured at the same event. It was on this occasion that Jr. made his dry remark that the "duty of the scholar in this country is to make poverty respectable."[15]

When Jr. noted that his father partly supported himself by "writing a number of books," he was referring to Sr.'s famous "Breakfast Table" column in *The Atlantic Monthly*, his medical essays, his novels, his poetry. Holmes Jr. wrote just one book, but it was immensely influential: *The Common Law*, published in 1881 and still in publication today.[16]

Years later, Justice Holmes remembered his father's excitement when the postman delivered a parcel of books at their summer house in the Berkshires. "I was born and bred among them," father said of books, "and have the easy feeling,

---

[14] White, *Justice Oliver Wendell Holmes*, 7.
[15] Howe, *Justice Oliver Wendell Holmes*, vol. II, *The Proving Years*, 257–258.
[16] Oliver Wendell Holmes, Jr., *The Common Law* Rev. Ed. (New York, 2004).

when I get into their presence, that a stable boy has among horses."[17] Like father, like son.

Sr. and Jr. loved to chase fires together too. Fires fascinated Jr. for the rest of his life. It may not be too much of a stretch to say that Holmes's utterances – about "falsely shouting fire in a crowded theater," and, in a Memorial Day address in 1881, "Through our great good fortune, in our youth our hearts were touched with fire" — were metaphors for his interest in fires.

So, though Holmes Sr.'s "laboratory" for son Holmes Jr. was not as comprehensive or deliberate as James Mill's for his son, the influence of OWH Sr. and his Brahmin milieu was profound.

Biographers of Holmes have seemed to downplay the immense contribution to Justice Holmes's makeup added by his mother, Amelia Lee Jackson Holmes. In the early 1850's, for example, when Wendell was growing into his teens, the two of them took long walks together near their house at Pittsfield.[18] It was his mother who listened to him recite his grammar lessons. It was his mother who later drilled him for his bar exam. During the Civil War, when Wendell suffered his third wound, getting shot in the heel, it was his mother he wrote to first, not his father. Later, it was his mother he asked to help him decide which of his Civil War letters should be destroyed.[19]

---

[17] Oliver Wendell Holmes, *The Works of Oliver Wendell Holmes* (Boston, 1892), I, 131.
[18] Baker, *The Justice from Beacon Hill*, 64, 121.
[19] *Ibid.*, 64, 684n.

Holmes and his mother, c. 1856, presumably
at the Holmes's family house in Pittsfield, Massachusetts.
(*Courtesy of Historical & Special Collections, Harvard Law School Library. Record ID: olvwork389558*)

If young Wendell came home after a bender and was found the next morning sleeping at the front door, his father's teasing meant nothing compared to mother's devastating silence. Biographer John Monagan reports, "Justice Holmes told a Porcellian Club or A.D. Club audience that after getting tipsy at a club party in college, he staggered as far as the Holmeses' vestibule where he spent the remainder of the night and was found in the morning. His parents reacted in typical but opposite fashion: His father was voluble and caustic for weeks, but his mother never said a word — and that cut Wendell to the quick."[20]

Wendell asserted that he acquired not just his skepticism from his mother, but also a penchant for deep melancholy.[21] Just shy of his 90th birthday Holmes asked, "Why not be content with pleasure? I can't answer, except that by my experiences in life and more by the temperament I got from my mother, without some feeling of accomplishment I feel as if it were time for me to die."[22]

Wendell had happy moments with his siblings — brother Ned and sister Amelia, neither of whom seemed to thrive as much in the same family "laboratory" — but they appeared to be only occasionally close to him.

One other family member warrants mention — Uncle John Holmes, Dr. Holmes's affable, fun-loving brother, who delighted all extended-family Holmes members with his stories and his cursing.[23] Uncle John was a Brahmin too, attended Harvard Law School, and practiced law. Justice Holmes's biographer Mark DeWolfe Howe found evidence that it might have been Uncle John who talked nephew Wendell into a career in law.[24]

---

[20] Monagan, *The Grand Panjandrum*, 25.
[21] Holmes to Morris Cohen, February 5, 1919, in Felix Cohen, "Holmes-Cohen Correspondence," *Journal of the History of Ideas* 9 (1948): 3, 14–15; White, *Justice Oliver Wendell Holmes,* 16, 494–495n; Baker, *The Justice from Beacon Hill,* 42.
[22] Howe (ed.), *Holmes-Laski Letters,* II, 1278; Howe, *Justice Oliver Wendell Holmes,* I, *The Shaping Years,* 280n.
[23] Baker, *The Justice from Beacon Hill,* 66.
[24] Howe, *Justice Oliver Wendell Holmes,* I, *The Shaping Years,* 177.

Wendell's family was not the only "laboratory" equipment shaping his remarkable talents. He grew up in one of the most rarefied neighborhoods of the nation. It does take a village, not just a family, to raise a child. For Wendell, the village was an extraordinary Brahmin Boston. Wendell's father invented the term "Brahmin" for Boston's caste around Beacon Hill.[25] He also invented the phrase "hub of the solar system" — as in John Updike's epic ode to one of baseball's greatest hitters, Ted Williams, a century later, "Hub Bids Kid Adieu" — for the Boston State House.[26]

In Brahmin Boston between 1859 and 1870, the Holmes family lived at 21 Charles Street, as noted earlier.[27] The office of publishers Ticknor and Fields, close by, became known as the "hub of the Hub." An astounding array of celebrated writers visited this office, some many times a day, including Wendell's famous father, plus Horatio Alger, Lydia Child, Charles Dickens, Sir Arthur Conan Doyle, Ralph Waldo Emerson, Nathaniel Hawthorne, Julia Ward Howe, Henry Wadsworth Longfellow, James Russell Lowell, Harriet Beecher Stowe, Alfred Tennyson, Henry David Thoreau, Mark Twain, John Greenleaf Whittier.[28]

---

[25] The term could have been borrowed from the Hindu caste system in India and the worship of a breed of domestic cattle. *See* the website *Celebrate Boston*, cf. "Boston Brahmin, Origin" http://www.celebrateboston.com/culture/brahmin-origin.htm.

[26] John Updike, "Hub Bids Kid Adieu," *The New Yorker*, October 22, 1960.

[27] Petronella (ed.), *Victorian Boston Today*, 241n.

[28] Mark A. DeWolfe Howe, *Holmes of the Breakfast Table* (Mamaroneck, New York, 1972), 4; Petronella (ed.), *Victorian Boston Today*, 125; R. Todd Felton, *A Journey into the Transcendentalists' New England*

During boyhood, young Holmes experienced such heady company west of Boston, too. Other literati mingled nearby "Holmesdale" — the Holmeses' summer house just south of Pittsfield [29] in the Berkshires — including the Emersons, the Longfellows, the Lowells, Harriet Beecher Stowe, Washington Irving, and Herman Melville and Nathaniel Hawthorne, two of Dr. Holmes's famous patients.[30]

Schooling for Wendell, like John Stuart Mill's, was anything but random. Wendell's parents picked elite schools that would prepare him for Harvard College. There was never any question that he would go to Harvard, a rite of passage for the Holmes family and Brahmin Boston. A dame's or nursery school, then T. R. Sullivan's elementary school in the historic Park Street Church's basement, and then Epes S. Dixwell's Latin school specifically calculated to prepare its pupils for Harvard — here, Holmes Jr.'s teachers supplemented his parents' enthusiasm for books, curiosity, ideas, writing.

From the earliest stages in the classroom, little Wendell was writing precocious notebook essays on Socrates, Alexander the Great, the Pilgrims, or the California gold rush. Schoolmaster Dixwell remembered the Holmes boy liked to walk with him to "talk of all topics."[31]

Before college, outside his schoolboy classrooms, Holmes began his lifelong habit of eclectic and voracious reading — not quite as early as John Stuart Mill's mandated regimen, but

---

(Berkeley, 2006), 28; Howe, *Justice Oliver Wendell Holmes*, I, *The Shaping Years*, 13–14.
[29] Petronella (ed.), *Victorian Boston Today*, 237n.
[30] Baker, *The Justice from Beacon Hill*, 54–55.
[31] White, *Justice Oliver Wendell Holmes*, 24; Baker, *The Justice from Beacon Hill*, 54, 69.

impressive nonetheless. Books were a crucial part of his upbringing. His brother, sister, and parents gave him books for his birthdays. Today you can check Holmes family sign-outs on the borrowing lists from the Boston Athenaeum — what Henry James called "the honored haunt of all the most civilized."[32]

Harvard College, as scornful contemporaries like Henry Adams and Henry Cabot Lodge attested, meant mostly boring classes and teachers. You could go through four years of Harvard College, wrote Adams, with nary a mention of Karl Marx or Auguste Comte — two writers who were turning the 19th century upside down.[33] But Holmes enjoyed its social clubs, like the Porcellian and the A.D. Club. He performed in at least three Hasty Pudding Show farces, and watched his brother Ned perform in later ones — not what you would expect from a "cold intellectual" portrayed by Holmes revisionists.[34]

Holmes Sr. surrounded the family with famous literary peerage from all over the world, like Emerson whom Wendell treated as a mentor, or Hawthorne, or Dickens, or Chicago's William Dean Howells. James Mill had done the same for his son.

And like the younger Mill, Wendell's youthful male friendships included a host of brilliant conversationalists. Henry and Brooks Adams, Chauncey Wright and John Fiske were among them.[35] Right after the Civil War, Holmes became

---

[32] Henry James, *American Scene* (London, 1907), 232.
[33] Henry Adams, *The Education of Henry Adams* (Cambridge, Massachusetts, 1918), 60; Baker, *The Justice from Beacon Hill*, 74.
[34] White, *Justice Oliver Wendell Holmes*, 27; Baker, *The Justice from Beacon Hill*, 192.
[35] Howe, *Justice Oliver Wendell Holmes*, I, *The Shaping Years*, 221.

296 Beacon Street, c. 1900, where Holmes and Fanny lived with his parents before 1875 and again after 1889.
(*Courtesy of Historical & Special Collections, Harvard Law School Library. Record ID: olvwork392114*)

especially close to William and Henry James. For a few years, they spent hours "twisting the tale of the cosmos" in philosophical discussions, including trips to New Hampshire. Eventually they drifted apart, as each of them pursued different professional interests — Henry became an expatriate writer in England, William wrote the classic 1902 study *Varieties of Religious Experience*, while Wendell buried himself in legal research.[36]

---

[36] White, *Justice Oliver Wendell Holmes*, 88–95, 103, 359.

By the 1870's, newlyweds Wendell and Fanny entertained occasional illustrious drop-ins like Oscar Wilde at their apartment above that drugstore at 10 Beacon Street. Summer guests like John Fiske, or Owen Wister — later the author of a kind of *Ivanhoe* western classic titled *The Virginian* — visited Wendell and Fanny at Buzzards Bay.[37] But aside from these budding luminaries, and aside from befriending senior law partners after finishing Harvard Law School, Holmes became a scholarly hermit. He gave up socializing altogether — except socializing with ideas — in his solitary research for what would become his seminal 1881 book *The Common Law*.

During and after the Civil War, Holmes also befriended several ladies, including his future wife and schoolmaster's daughter Fanny Dixwell. During his marriage with Fanny, she would be his best friend.

Much later in his life, according to his former secretary Francis Biddle, Holmes poked fun at himself for his intellectual friendships with women. He said, "The fun of talking with women ... was that they carried you away, so that you could express your innards with all the appropriate rapture, floating on the exquisite breath of your own egotism; reaching so far that suddenly you might look at her and say: 'By the way, my dear, what is your name?'"[38]

---

[37] Howe, *Justice Oliver Wendell Holmes*, II, *The Proving Years*, 253–255; Owen Wister, *Roosevelt: The Story of a Friendship, 1880–1919* (New York, 1930), 129.

[38] Francis Biddle, *Mr. Justice Holmes* (New York, 1946), 148–149. Another former secretary, Donald Hiss, remembered one woman saying that her friendship with Justice Holmes was casual and occasional, "but that

10 Beacon Street today, just beyond the Boston Athenaeum in the foreground, Boston, Massachusetts. Wendell's and Fanny's apartment was on the second floor, above that drugstore.
(*Courtesy of the authors*)

Arguably Holmes's most important friend at Harvard, male or female, was a Quaker from mainline Philadelphia — Norwood Penrose ("Pen") Hallowell — more important even than his Brahmin roommates at Mr. Danforth's private rooming house on Linden Street across from the Harvard Yard.[39] Hallowell attracted Wendell to abolitionism, even teaming up as bodyguards to deter the frequent disruptions at abolitionist speeches around Boston. Hallowell helped

---

voice ... I'll never forget that voice." See Monagan, *The Grand Panjandrum*, 23.

[39] Howe, *Justice Oliver Wendell Holmes*, I, *The Shaping Years*, 39, 292n.

persuade Holmes to drop out of Harvard in his final senior-year semester, to fight together in the Civil War.[40] Chivalry, in an age when Rudyard Kipling and Sir Walter Scott's *Ivanhoe* were immensely popular — Mark Twain once referred to it as "the Sir Walter disease" [41] — and independence, for Holmes Jr. from Holmes Sr., seemed to demand leaving Harvard early to fight in the Civil War.

---

[40] Holmes-Lewis Einstein letter of April 17, 1914 in James B. Peabody (ed.), *Holmes-Einstein Letters* (New York, 1964), 89; White, *Justice Oliver Wendell Holmes,* 31.

[41] Mark Twain (Samuel Clemens), *Life on the Mississippi,* in *Mississippi Writings* (1883; reprint, New York, 1982), 501.

Major Oliver Wendell Holmes, Jr., of Co. A and Co. G,
20th Massachusetts Infantry Regiment in uniform with sword.
Silsbee, Case & Co., photographer.
(*Courtesy of Library of Congress*)

4

CIVIL WAR

"Through our great good fortune, in our youth our hearts were touched with fire."[1]

HOLMES BELIEVED THAT his wartime experiences molded his thought and character in significant ways. Beyond doubt his military service imbued him with a strong sense of duty that he would retain throughout his long life. His wife Fanny once teased that had it not been for the Civil War, Wendell would have been a "coxcomb."[2]

Holmes was impelled to join the Army, and to give all of his strength to the Union cause, even though young men of his generation and social class were not expected to do so. Many of his contemporaries at Harvard joined the Confederate side, or did not join at all.

Later he said the Army taught that "there were situations... in which I was inferior to men I might have looked down upon had not the experience taught me to look up."[3] Holmes witnessed and experienced brutality, horrific

---

[1] Oliver Wendell Holmes, Jr., "Memorial Day," Keene, New Hampshire, May 30, 1884, in Mark DeWolfe Howe (comp.), *The Occasional Speeches of Justice Oliver Wendell Holmes* (Cambridge, Massachusetts, 1962), 4; White, *Justice Oliver Wendell Holmes*, 49, 502n.
[2] Baker, *The Justice from Beacon Hill*, 105.
[3] Howe (ed.), *Holmes-Laski Letters*, II, 905.

loss of life to gain a military objective, physical hardship, exhaustion, dysentery, hunger, thirst, and serial incompetence. These conditions doubtless contributed to his sense of fate and self-reliance. He may have become a pragmatist on the battlefield. The only question for the young officer was, how can I do this job and do it now? General principles had no application in war. Life was cheap on the front lines.

Lieutenant Oliver Wendell Holmes, Jr., Nov. 11, 1862.
(*Courtesy of Historical & Special Collections, Harvard Law School Library. Record ID: olvwork384983*)

The handsome young man who was so eager to join the fight in 1861, is seen in pictures as a tall, slender, clean-shaven soldier, resplendent in his officer's uniform. Look at pictures of him seventy years later, in the 1930's, and the same face emerges like a palimpsest beneath the large moustache and hair, now white but still abundant and falling across his brow.

Justice Oliver Wendell Holmes, Jr., March 1931.
(*Courtesy of Historical & Special Collections, Harvard Law School Library. Record ID: olvwork389858*)

Holmes would leave the army satisfied he had done his duty, an idea that was of paramount importance to him. His letters home during the war spoke of his satisfaction that in battle he had acted "very cool and did my duty I am sure."[4] The responsibility to do his duty was a trait that would remain with him as a guiding principle for the rest of his life. He took great pride in his regiment, writing, "I really very

---

[4] Mark DeWolfe Howe (ed.), *Touched with Fire: Civil War Letters and Diary of Oliver Wendell Holmes, Jr.* (New York, 2000 edition), xii–xiii.

much doubt whether there is any Regt wh. can compare with ours in the Army of the Potomac."[5] All armies attempt to imbue the individual soldier with a sense of collective pride, the idea that the individual is a member of a unified organism, expected to act with selfless devotion and sacrifice as may be necessary for the whole to achieve victory. Holmes learned this lesson and was proud he had.

He saw his friends die and suffer terribly. When Henry L. Abbott, one of Holmes's closest friends, was killed at Fredericksburg, Holmes wrote that if Abbott had lived he "would have been a master and leader," and "[i]n action he was sublime."[6] Second Lieutenant Sumner Paine, Holmes's first cousin, was killed at Gettysburg on July 3, 1863.[7]

Holmes would never forget what he described as "the shrieking fragments [that] go tearing through your company," or "feeling your foot slip upon a dead man's body during picket-line duty at night in a black and unknown wood."[8]

If Holmes ever had religious beliefs, he certainly abandoned them after experiencing the slaughter of war. The paradox — and good fortune — of Holmes's wartime experience is that he dedicated himself to the community necessary for battle while emerging as one of the most original thinkers in the nation's history.

---

[5] *Ibid.*, xviii.
[6] *Ibid.*, xiii.
[7] *Ibid.*, 92, n. 2.
[8] Holmes, "The Soldier's Faith," delivered Memorial Day 1895 to Harvard seniors. Quoted in Max Lerner (ed.), *The Mind and Faith of Justice Holmes: His Speeches, Essays, Letters, and Judicial Opinions* (New York, 1943), 20–21; White, *Justice Oliver Wendell Holmes*, 81.

Holmes wrote his parents describing physical battlefield privations which, in another context, may have seemed trivial but that were matters of life or death in war.

He was a fighter. He sustained wounds in three battles, two of them life-threatening.

The Battle of Ball's Bluff was fought in October 1861 in Virginia, about 25 miles northwest of Washington on the Potomac River. Near Leesburg, the bank of the river "reared up tall there, over 100 feet, steep and mean-looking; Ball's Bluff it was called. ..."[9] Prominent men at the battle in addition to Holmes, described as the son of the celebrated Oliver Wendell Holmes, included a grandson of Paul Revere and a nephew of James Russell Lowell.[10]

On October 21, the twenty-year-old lieutenant was shot twice. In a letter to his mother on October 23, he described the battle.

> I was out in front of our men encouraging 'em on when a spent shot knocked the wind out of me & I fell — then I crawled to the rear a few paces & rose by help of the 1st Sergt; & the Colonel who was passing said 'That's right Mr. Holmes — Go to the Rear' but I felt that I couldn't without more excuse so up I got and rushed to the front where hearing the Col. cheering the men on I waved my sword and asked if none would follow me when down I went again by the Colonel's side.[11]

---

[9] Shelby Foote, *The Civil War: A Narrative* (New York, 1958), I, 104.
[10] *Ibid.*, 108.
[11] Howe (ed.), *Touched with Fire*, 13.

The second shot was by a ball that entered his left side and came out on the right side of his chest.[12] He was certain he was dying, but later wrote in his diary that he had resisted the temptation to make a "deathbed recantation" which would have been "a cowardly way of giving way to fear."[13]

Nearly a year later, on September 17, 1862, Holmes sustained his second wound. The battle on that day was named for a "rust-brown creek called Antietam Creek."[14] It was only about forty miles from Ball's Bluff.

The Battle of Antietam would be the bloodiest day of fighting in American history. The dead and wounded on the Union side were 14,756 men and on the Confederate 13,609, a total of over 28,000 men.[15] At the famous cornfield, Union General Joe Hooker's men "ran into blinding sheets of flame."[16] The Union troops were said to be "[t]oo tightly wedged to maneuver as a unit, or even dodge as individuals, men fell in windrows, the long files writhing like wounded snakes."[17]

Holmes, then a captain, wrote to his parents at 3 a.m. on September 17, just hours before the great battle. Writing by "Candle light," he simply noted, "We have not been in any recent fight."

The next day, writing his parents of what he regarded as his "usual luck," he described his wound: a ball had entered his neck "at the rear passing straight through the central seam

---

[12] *Ibid.*

[13] *Ibid.*, 27–28.

[14] Foote, *The Civil War*, I, 682.

[15] *Ibid.*, 682, 702; *The Civil War: A Film by Ken Burns* (September, 1990).

[16] Foote, *The Civil War*, I, 688.

[17] *Ibid.*, 692.

of coat and waistcoat collar coming out to the front on the left hand side."[18] One eminent historian wrote, "Severely wounded and left for dead in this action was a young captain in the 20th Massachusetts, Oliver Wendell Holmes, Jr."[19]

At the end of the day on September 17, "[n]ight fell on a scene of horror beyond imagining. Nearly 6,000 men lay dead or dying, and another 17,000 wounded groaned in agony or endured in silence. The casualties at Antietam numbered four times the total suffered by American soldiers at the Normandy beaches on June 6, 1944. More than twice as many Americans lost their lives in one day...as fell in combat in the War of 1812, the Mexican War and the Spanish-American war *combined*."[20] By comparison, in the horrific attacks on America on September 11, 2001, there were just under 3,000 deaths.

Fortunately, Holmes found cover with numerous other wounded Union soldiers in a small farmhouse.[21]

The horror of battle was occasionally marked with generosity among the enemies. Holmes's college friend Pen Hallowell took cover in the same house that Holmes found. Hallowell wrote that a Confederate soldier put his head

---

[18] Howe (ed.), *Touched with Fire*, 64.
[19] James M. McPherson, *Battle Cry of Freedom: The Civil War Era* (New York, 1988), 541.
[20] *Ibid.*, 544.
[21] This may have been the "stone cottage surrounded by more than 300 acres of pasture and woods ... used as a hospital during the Battle of Antietam, later owned by the family of Laura Hillenbrand, celebrated author of the books *Seabiscuit* and *Unbroken*." (Wil S. Hylton, "The Unbreakable Laura Hillenbrand," *The New York Times*, December 21, 2014, pp. 31–40). Called the "Nicodemus house" in Howe (ed.), *Touched with Fire*, 65n.

through a window of the house where he and Holmes were lying, asked if the wounded were thirsty and tossed his canteen to them. He left to resume the battle against the Yankees, and returned about fifteen minutes later saying he needed his canteen.[22]

Holmes told a doctor who was dressing his neck wound, "I'm devilish glad it ain't a case for amputation...for I haven't much confidence in your skill as a surgeon."[23] To a woman who was helping care for the wounded in the house he dictated a letter to his father in Latin.[24] Obviously, the volunteer nurse was herself a remarkable person.

Holmes's letters often described deaths and amputated limbs of friends, but also gamely spoke of his own high spirits.

Holmes's strained relationship with his father, Dr. Holmes, was reflected in a December 20, 1862 letter to his father whom he addressed as "My Dear Governor." His father had held forth on his views of the war from the safety of Boston. Holmes upbraided him in the letter, saying, "I think you are hopeful [of a Union victory] because (excuse me) you are ignorant." He then signed, "Your Aff. Son, O W Holmes, Jr."[25] In March 1863 he wrote to "My Dear Dad," telling his father that son would "let bygones be bygones — if you will."[26]

On May 3, 1863, Holmes informed his mother he had suffered a third wound at 2nd Fredericksburg. A cannon was

---

[22] Howe (ed.), *Touched with Fire*, 65, n. 1.
[23] *Ibid.*, 66.
[24] *Ibid.*, 67–68.
[25] *Ibid.*, 79–81.
[26] *Ibid.*, 86.

brought up to an earthwork and trained on Holmes's company which was "exactly in range — 1st discharge puff — second puff (as the shell burst) and my knapsack supporter is knocked to pieces (Mem. We are lying down) 2nd discharge man in front of me hit — 3d whang the iron enters through garter and shoe into my heel — later I've been chloroformed & had bone extracted — probably shant lose foot."[27]

Laudanum bottle, 1861-1864, given to Oliver Wendell Holmes, Jr., by his father, Dr. Oliver Wendell Holmes, Sr., when he enlisted in the Union Army.
(*Courtesy of Historical & Special Collections, Harvard Law School Library. Record ID: olvwork411503*)

Holmes refused promotion to lieutenant colonel in favor of a staff position which he thought would be safer. But in May 1864 he narrowly escaped capture as a staff officer. He wrote to his parents on May 16, 1864 saying he would "stay on the staff if possible till the end of the campaign and then if

---

[27] *Ibid.*, 92.

I am still alive, I shall resign."[28] The letter gave rise to another testy exchange with his father who apparently wrote his son questioning his intention. Holmes answered, "I am sure I cannot have conveyed the idea, rightfully, that I intended resigning before the campaign was over…I must say I dislike such a misunderstanding, so discreditable to my feeling of soldierly honor."[29]

According to a war correspondent, in July 1864 Holmes's 20th Massachusetts Regiment departed the Army on expiration of its service. The correspondent wrote that "Captain Holmes served more than two years steadily and chivalrously as a line officer, was three times severely wounded, and in this campaign has been zealous and indefatigable as a member of the Sixth Corps staff, has always been conspicuously daring and capably efficient and he goes out of service because his regiment does, not because he would taste the sweets of home and Boston."[30] Historian James M. McPherson confirmed that "Holmes did not resign; he served out the full three years of his enlistment, and returned home with honor in July 1864."[31]

On September 18, 1863, Holmes's friend Henry L. Abbott wrote to his father Josiah G. Abbott:

> I am glad you are going to take Holmes under your wing. His father, of course, one can't help despising. But Oliver

---

[28] *Ibid.*, 122.
[29] *Ibid.*, 135.
[30] *Ibid.*, 149, n. 3.
[31] James M. McPherson, "The Monstrous War," *New York Review of Books* (July 10, 2014): 69.

Junior, though you have an instinctive dislike to his speculative nature, is infinitely more manly than the little conceited Doctor ... [A] man here in the hardships and dangers of the field can easily detach what is base in a man's character, and it is particularly trying to Holmes who is a student rather than a man of action. But since I have seen him intimately, he has always been most cool, cheerful, and self sacrificing. ... He is considered in the army a remarkably brave and well instructed officer, who has stuck to his work, though wounded often enough to discourage any but an honorable gentleman.[32]

1869 Boston reunion of the Officers of the Twentieth Regiment, Massachusetts Volunteers Left to right: Gen. Francis W. Palfrey; Lt. Col. O. W. Holmes, Jr.; Gen. Edward N. Hallowell; Maj. Gen. William F. Bartlett; Gen. Charles L. Peirson; Capt. Edward F. Robins; Col. William Raymond Lee; Gen. George N. Macy; Gen. Charles A. Whittier; Capt. John C. Putnam; Capt. Henry W. T. Mali; Capt. C. Linsee Tilden; Lt. Nathaniel T. Messer; Capt. N. P. Hallowell.
(*Courtesy of Historical & Special Collections, Harvard Law School Library. Record ID: olvwork389561*)

---

[32] Howe, *Justice Oliver Wendell Holmes*, I, *The Shaping Years*, 158 and 158n.

The war changed Holmes, as it would change anyone. No longer did he see life through the lens of the privileged world of Beacon Hill. Life itself, he thought, is a struggle akin to war. The dominant power wins, the weaker loses. He accepted this equation, indeed insisted on it. His thinking and his legal opinions reflected it.

Thirty years after the War had ended, Holmes gave a Memorial Day address in which he said he did not know what was true and did not know the meaning of the universe. Continuing, he said:

> But in the midst of doubt, in the collapse of creeds, there is one thing I do not doubt, that no man who lives in the same world with most of us can doubt, and that is that the faith is true and adorable which leads a soldier to throw away his life in obedience to a blindly accepted duty, in a cause which he little understands, in a plan of campaign of which he has no notion, under tactics of which he does not see the use.[33]

The profound impact that the Civil War had on Holmes, and his deep sense of duty arising from it, are evident here. Holmes shared this "blindly accepted duty" as he repeatedly demonstrated during the War. He had no faith in religion, unless his concept of duty might loosely be called his religion. He knew that he did not understand the origin or the reason he was driven to obey such a duty. But he also knew that this was the kind of faith he had.

---

[33] Francis Biddle, *Justice Holmes, Natural Law, and the Supreme Court* (New York, 1961), 15.

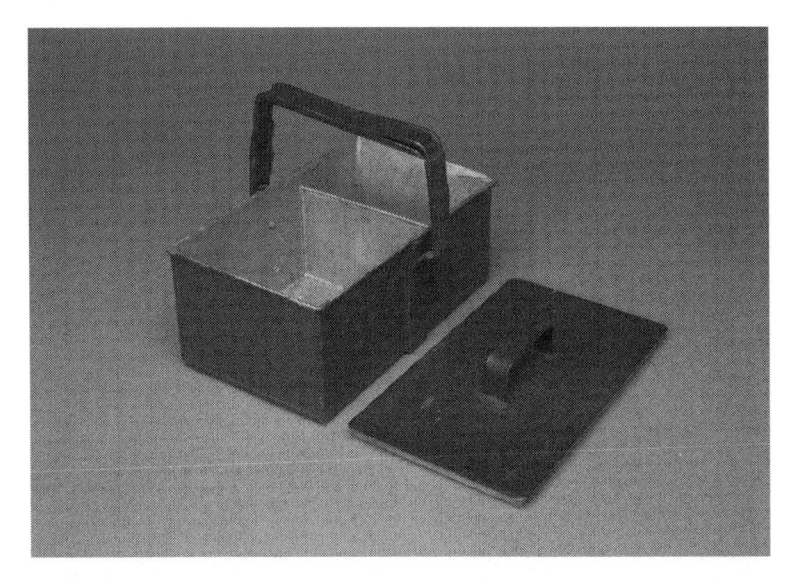

Lunchbox: Painted tin ammunition box used as a lunchbox by Justice Oliver Wendell Holmes, Jr., when he served on the United States Supreme Court, 1902–1932. Since the Supreme Court had no separate building and the justices no offices, they had to carry their box lunches to their restricted court room and robing room on the ground floor of the Capitol.
(*Courtesy of Historical & Special Collections, Harvard Law School Library. Record ID: olvwork416285*)

In a 1923 letter to his young friend Dr. John C. Wu, Holmes said:

> I remember just before the battle of Antietam thinking and perhaps saying to a brother officer that it would be easy after a comfortable breakfast to come down the steps of one's house pulling on one's gloves and smoking a cigar to get on a horse and charge a battery up Beacon Street, while the ladies waved handkerchiefs from a balcony. But the reality was to pass a night on the ground in the rain with your bowels out of order and then after no particular breakfast to wade a stream and attack the enemy. That is life.[34]

---

[34] *Ibid.*, 14.

THE COMMON LAW.

LECTURE I.

EARLY FORMS OF LIABILITY.

THE object of this book is to present a general view of the Common Law. To accomplish the task, other tools are needed besides logic. It is something to show that the consistency of a system requires a particular result, but it is not all. The life of the law has not been logic: it has been experience. The felt necessities of the time, the prevalent moral and political theories, intuitions of public policy, avowed or unconscious, even the prejudices which judges share with their fellow-men, have had a good deal more to do than the syllogism in determining the rules by which men should be governed. The law embodies the story of a nation's development through many centuries, and it cannot be dealt with as if it contained only the axioms and corollaries of a book of mathematics. In order to know what it is, we must know what it has been, and what it tends to become. We must alternately consult history and existing theories of legislation. But the most difficult labor will be to understand the combination of the two into new products at every stage. The substance of the law at any given time pretty nearly

Holmes's annotated copy of *The Common Law* (1881), "Early Forms of Liability," p. 1, with marginalia in Oliver Wendell Holmes, Jr's. hand.
(Courtesy of *Historical & Special Collections, Harvard Law School Library. Hollis Record ID: 0099283*)

5

DEFINING LAW

"The life of the law has not been logic: it has been experience."

A MAJOR INGREDIENT of Holmes's thought was his skepticism. He questioned everything, accepted nothing on faith, including his own ideas. He looked at issues and ideas with an "Olympian detachment."[1] His restless mind, like a scalpel, probed and challenged the truth of every proposition that he encountered. He had no use for generalities. He has been called "a philosopher who considered all philosophic systems inadequate."[2]

Holmes did not merely study American law; he defined it. More than any other thinker in our history, Holmes's thought has influenced the development of the law in this country.

In a series of twelve lectures Holmes gave at the Lowell Institute in Boston, he began the task of defining law. He then rewrote his ideas, enlarged upon them, then published the final version in his 1881 book *The Common Law*.

The book changed our understanding of American law forever. Over a century later, the work of legal scholars, judges, lawyers, philosophers, and historians have been influenced by Holmes's thought, whether consciously or not. His ideas are

---

[1] Gerald Gunther, *Learned Hand: The Man and the Judge* (Cambridge, Massachusetts, 1994), 345.
[2] Biddle, *Justice Holmes, Natural Law, and the Supreme Court*, 5.

woven into the tapestry of American law that exists today. "The book became famous all over the world. ..."[3]

Holmes's genius for expressing his thoughts with concise eloquence is on display in his book. As he would later do as a judge, he began his book *The Common Law* with an arresting statement. In the fourth sentence on page 1, he announced a doctrine that is fully alive and often quoted today: "The life of the law has not been logic: it has been experience." Holmes the pragmatist was describing what actually happened in courtrooms in 1881 and still happens today. He then seized the essence of law:

> The felt necessities of the time, the prevalent moral and political theories, intuitions of public policy, avowed or unconscious, even the prejudices which judges share with their fellow-men, have had a good deal more to do than the syllogism in determining the rules by which men should be governed.[4]

In the book that followed, Holmes traced the history of law, its branches into subjects such as criminal law, torts, fraud, contract. The sheer depth of his learning at his young age — he was just under forty when he wrote the book — strikes the reader with wonder. Holmes examined and connected to our law the ancient laws of Greece, Rome, England, Germany, Scotland, and numerous others. He did so in clear, accessible prose.

---

[3] *Ibid.*, 13.
[4] Holmes, *The Common Law*, 1.

In January 1897, Holmes delivered an address at the dedication of a new hall of the Boston University School of Law. The address was published later that year in an article in the *Harvard Law Review*, called "The Path of the Law."[5] Along with his earlier book *The Common Law*, the article set forth Holmes's unique and ground-breaking definition of the law. Characteristically, he began by making clear that the law is not an abstract notion. He immediately reduced the definition to its most concrete level:

> When we study law we are not studying a mystery but a well known profession. We are studying what we shall want in order to appear before judges, or to advise people in such a way as to keep them out of court. ... The object of our study, then, is prediction. We study the law books of this country and in England, extending back for six hundred years...In these sibylline leaves are gathered the scattered prophesies of the past upon the cases in which the axe will fall. These are what properly have been called the oracles of the law. ...

Decades later, as a Supreme Court justice, Holmes would return to his idea that the law is not a "mystery." In typically incisive brevity, he captured the same idea: "The common law," he wrote, "is not a brooding omnipresence in the sky. ..."[6]

In "The Path of the Law," Holmes said:

---

[5] Oliver Wendell Holmes, Jr., "The Path of the Law," *Harvard Law Review* 10 (1897): 457.
[6] *Southern Pacific Co. v. Jensen*, 244 U.S. 205, 222 (1917).

You will find some text writers telling you that it is something different from what is decided by the courts of Massachusetts or England, that it is a system of reason, that it is a deduction from principles of ethics or admitted axioms or what not.[7]

Holmes did not agree with these text writers. "The prophecies of what the courts will do in fact, and nothing more pretentious, are what I mean by law."[8] To illustrate his idea, he used "the bad man" metaphor. What does a legal rule mean to a bad man? "Mainly, and in the first place, a prophecy that if he does certain things he will be subjected to disagreeable consequences...."[9] That is the only legal question that interests the bad man. What will keep me out of jail? Or what will prevent me from being sued, or from paying if a suit is successful? The bad man cares nothing about legal principle. He is interested only in how the law will affect him.

Holmes closed his address with some advice:

To an imagination of any scope the most far-reaching form of power is not money, it is the command of ideas. If you want great examples read Mr. Leslie Stephen's "History of English Thought in the Eighteenth Century," and see how a hundred years after his death the abstract speculation of Descartes had become a practical force controlling the conduct of men. Read the works of the great German jurists, and see how much more the world is governed to-day [sic]

---

[7] Holmes, "The Path of the Law," 460.
[8] *Ibid.*, 461.
[9] *Ibid.*

by Kant than by Bonaparte. ... The remoter and more general aspects of the law are those which give it universal interest. It is through them that you not only become a great master in your calling, but connect your subject with the universe and catch an echo of the infinite, a glimpse of its unfathomable process, a hint of the universal law.[10]

Of course, Holmes's "bad man" cares nothing about "catching a hint of the universal law." That was Holmes's point. Whether they recognize it or not, the bad man, the judges deciding cases, and the lawyers advising clients and trying the cases, have inherited the "postponed power" of 600 years of struggle to reach an understanding of what the law is. That inheritance is the basis for predicting and deciding "where the axe will fall."

When Holmes asserted that "the life of the law has not been logic: it has been experience," he began not just an idea, but a movement, now called "sociological jurisprudence." Holmes's lectures and book called on judges in deciding cases to take into account non-legal considerations such as social and economic data, which Holmes called the "felt necessities of the time." Holmes and Roscoe Pound were "the great theorists of sociological jurisprudence, but Louis Brandeis would be its great practitioner. In 1908 when he submitted his path-breaking brief in *Muller v. Oregon*,[11] Brandeis put into practice the theory that he had heard Holmes talk about more than a quarter century earlier."[12]

---

[10] *Ibid.*, 478.
[11] 208 U.S. 412.
[12] Melvin I. Urofsky, *Louis D. Brandeis: A Life* (New York, 2009), 76n.

In *Muller*, the Supreme Court upheld the validity of an Oregon law forbidding the employment of women in factories or laundries for more than 10 hours per day. The Court recognized that, "In the brief filed by Mr. Louis D. Brandeis, ... is a very copious collection of all these matters." The Court said, "The legislation and opinions referred to ... may not be, technically speaking, authorities, ... yet they are significant of a widespread belief that women's physical structure, and the functions she performs in consequence thereof, justify special legislation restricting or qualifying the conditions under which she should be permitted to toil." The Court concluded, "We take judicial cognizance of all matters of general knowledge." Since then Brandeis's submission has been known as the "Brandeis Brief."

Thus, by this circuitous route, did Holmes's ideas, expressed decades earlier, take root in the law.

Like his father in 1833 studying medicine in Paris, and grandfather Abiel in 1800 compiling his *Annals of America*,[13] Holmes had no use for dogma of any variety, especially unchallenged faith. He believed in facts and evidence, but philosophically questioned their very existence. He wrote that a legal proposition "grows more precise when we wash it in cynical acid. ..."[14] He accepted no proposition on faith. He challenged them all.

Not surprisingly, Holmes has been widely attacked by adherents to religions and other dogmatic theories based not on evidence but on blind faith. Believers in "natural law" —

---

[13] White, *Justice Oliver Wendell Holmes*, 10, 19.
[14] Holmes, "The Path of the Law," 457, 462.

an idea largely religious in origin, the theory that there is a set of laws that are "higher" and more "transcendent" than man-made law — regard Holmes as their enemy, a hated and dangerous figure whose views threaten their own most fundamental beliefs. "Men to a great extent believe what they want to," Holmes wrote, "although I see in that no basis for a philosophy that tells us what we should want to want."[15]

Holmes had particular disdain for judges who believe, and even apply, natural or religious law in deciding cases. Addressing that issue, Holmes said, "Jurists who believe in natural law seem to me to be in that naïve state of mind that accepts what has been familiar and accepted by them and their neighbors as something that must be accepted by all men everywhere."[16] But the notion that "our truth is cosmic truth" was entirely unfounded. "The law," he said on several occasions, "is not a brooding omnipresence in the sky."

Holmes even challenged the idea that there is a "right" to life. He said, "The right to life is sacrificed without a scruple, not only in war, but whenever the interest of society, that is, of the predominant power in the community, is thought to demand it." At that point, he wrote, "the sanctity disappears." Holmes did not argue that this state of affairs *should* prevail. He said it *did* prevail. Speaking of the idea of religion-based natural law, Holmes thought a "facile faith in design is the tap-root of most indifference to reality."[17]

---

[15] Justice Oliver Wendell Holmes, "Natural Law," *Harvard Law Review* 32 (1918): 40 ff.
[16] *Ibid.*, 41.
[17] Howe (ed.), *Holmes-Laski Letters*, I, 141.

Not surprisingly such views stimulated attacks by purveyors of dogma. Some superficial observers have called him a "cold, inhumane intellectual." These people are superficial because no fair-minded person can have read much about Holmes and reached this conclusion. His contemporaries would deliver the opposite verdict. They loved Holmes. They knew of his keen wit, his gentleness, his care in trying not to offend colleagues when he disagreed with them, his large community of close friends, his gentlemanly manners, both in and out of court. Read Holmes's hundreds of letters to friends and see how the real personal qualities of Holmes emerge.

Holmes loved witty stories. There are numerous examples. In a letter to his English friend Harold Laski he wrote, interspersed with a philosophical discussion: "You know the tale of the little boy who was told that God made everything. 'Did he make elephants?' 'Yes.' 'Did he make cows?' 'Yes.' 'Did he make flies?' 'Yes.' 'Fiddling work making flies I should think.'"[18]

In a letter to Felix Frankfurter, Holmes told another tale:

There was a young lady from Joppa
Who came in society cropper
She went to Ostend with a military friend
The rest of the story is not proper.[19]

---

[18] *Ibid.*, 219, Nov. 3, 1919.
[19] Robert M. Mennel and Christine L. Compston (eds.), *Holmes and Frankfurter: Their Correspondence, 1912–1934* (Durham, New Hampshire, 1996), Dec. 23, 1930.

For those who cast Holmes as a "cold intellectual," consider the following: Shortly after the Civil War, Captain Holmes and friends were about to climb Mt. Kearsarge in New Hampshire. Among those seeing them off was a little girl named Olivia Murray, who desperately wanted to go along.

> The Captain, catching sight of the child ... "Mrs. Murray, will you let Olivia come with us? I will take care of her."

Captain Holmes diverted the child with stories.

> Afterwards, little Olivia gratefully spent many weeks of arduous labor making a bookmark which she sent him, scarcely daring to hope that he would use it. Years passed before they saw each other again.

All these years later, Holmes was a senior Justice of the U.S. Supreme Court, living at 1720 Eye Street in Washington, D.C. Olivia was now Mrs. Bayard Cutting, and she came to tea, served downstairs. Then Justice Holmes said,

> he wanted Olivia to see his study and his books and took her upstairs. As they passed through his secretary's room, he asked the secretary to look on such and such a shelf and bring him a particular book. Out of it he took the bookmark the child had made for him and which he had kept and used for more than sixty years.[20]

---

[20] Howe, I, *Justice Oliver Wendell Holmes: The Shaping Years*, 202, 202n; in 1947 Judge Learned Hand told this story to Howe.

Erwin N. Griswold, later to serve as dean of Harvard Law School, told a story of Holmes that occurred in about 1930, just a few years before Holmes died. Griswold's mother visited her son in Washington, D.C. During the visit, Griswold said, "I told her of my admiration for Holmes." When she got back to Cleveland, the mother wrote to Holmes, "thanking him for the inspiration he provided for a young lawyer, her son." Then about ninety years of age, Holmes responded in longhand, saying that he greatly valued what she had written for, in his words, "If you become a minority of one, they lock you up." Griswold said, "I still have that letter, carefully protected in the pages of my copy of *The Common Law*."[21]

People who had known and worked with Holmes were often appalled by the sheer ignorance of some of the assaults on his views. One was a law clerk who had worked with Holmes a few years after Holmes took his position on the Supreme Court.

Francis Biddle was a preeminent legal figure who had been Holmes's secretary — today called a law clerk — in 1911-1912 following his graduation from Harvard Law School. Biddle would go on to distinguish himself in an illustrious legal career. After practicing law for 25 years he became a judge of the Circuit Court of Appeals for the Third Circuit, Solicitor General of the United States, and a member of the International Military Tribunal at Nuremberg.

---

[21] Griswold, "Foreword," in Novick (ed.), *Collected Works of Justice Holmes*, xv.

Biddle gave a series of lectures he published in a small book, *Justice Holmes, Natural Law, and the Supreme Court*. Before discussing the attacks, Biddle made clear:

> That I loved and admired Justice Holmes makes it difficult for me to resist this opportunity to talk about him and his detractors. But this is not merely a matter of coming to the defense of a great man whom little men are trying to pull down. Holmes's contribution to law — his insistence on examining objectively the facts which explain its life and its direction — involves keeping open the doors of the mind in a world which increasingly, I feel, is closing about us. The attacks are leveled against the emancipation of law from superstition — a task to which everything in Holmes was dedicated.[22]

Biddle, in particular, addressed attacks on Holmes by proponents of natural law. He said that priests, who read Holmes's letters, which were published a few years after Holmes's death, "wrote much of the criticism." Biddle thought the priests "must have spent many hours combing the letters to sustain their view that here was a modern antichrist worthy of their mettle."[23]

Holmes, Biddle said, was a "religious skeptic. His detractors could not concede that anyone who rejected God could be a good man."[24] Biddle wrote:

---

[22] Biddle, *Justice Holmes, Natural Law, and the Supreme Court*, 30–31.
[23] *Ibid.*, 27.
[24] *Ibid.*, 34.

The concentrated criticism of Holmes began in 1941 when the Reverend Francis E. Lucey, S.J., a writer who theretofore had been, comparatively speaking, unknown, published an article in *Social Science* called "Jurisprudence and the Future Social Order" ... Father John C. Ford, S.J., in the same year addressed the Jesuit Philosophical Association on "The Fundamentals of Holmes's Juristic Philosophy."[25]

Other Jesuits joined. As Biddle pointed out, in general their assaults were leveled at "the alien philosophies of Kant, Hume, Herbert Spencer, John Stuart Mill, Hobbes, Marx, and now Holmes [who] were 'cutting away at the foundations of American jurisprudence,' and might 'topple the superstructure which we are proud and happy to call our American Way of Life.'"[26]

Continuing, Biddle pointed out:

The charges against Holmes are about the same in all the articles and addresses: he was a skeptic and cynic who believed in no God and had no principles; he considered that law was nothing but the use of force, and that might makes right; he discarded all absolutes, including natural law, and defined truth as the vote of the majority; and he described morals as nothing but a curb on the normal human inclination to get your feet in the trough.[27]

Father John C. Ford, S.J., "... had been brought up, theologically speaking, on St. Thomas Aquinas and his

---

[25] *Ibid.*, 33.
[26] *Ibid.*
[27] *Ibid.*, 34.

doctrine that *all* law is based on natural law implanted by God in man."[28]

As seen, Holmes had no use and found no basis for natural law. The attacks on Holmes were gross distortions of his actual views, most likely intentional. Holmes did not claim that law was nothing but physical force. Nor did he say law *should* be based on force. As Biddle pointed out:

> What Holmes did say — and repeated in various ways — was that law was a *statement of the circumstances in which the public force will be brought to bear upon men through the courts*...When Holmes talked about law he always meant the same thing — the law that lawyers practice and judges declare, and from which human beings suffer; the law that permits a policeman to shoot an escaping felon, or a sheriff to manacle a kidnapper, or a judge to send a man to jail for refusing to testify. And in that sense law — what we call positive law — is based on force, and can hardly be said to exist unless it can be enforced.[29]

As Biddle accurately stressed, the priests, imbued with the notion of natural law, were following the theological claims of St. Thomas Aquinas, the 13th century Dominican priest and theologian who made natural law a cornerstone of Roman Catholic philosophy. In the centuries that followed, natural-law believers grounded their theories on religion-based theology, or simply found them to be "self-evident" — as Jefferson had in the Declaration of Independence. Such

---

[28] *Ibid.*, 35.
[29] *Ibid.*, 34–35.

"rights" were transcendent, endowed by a creator, divinely inspired and therefore higher than mere positive law created by humans. These sentiments, of course, had a highly self-serving dimension: they empowered the priest as a necessary intermediary between religion and worshipper.

Holmes's definition of law was what he *actually saw*. He was describing, not advocating, a simple point ignored by natural-law theorists. "Rights" were enforceable in the courts. This was not cynical. It was what the courts did day in and day out. In his view, as we have seen, "The law is not a brooding omnipresence in the sky." In his 1918 *Harvard Law Review* article "Natural Law,"[30] Holmes noted we all have impulses that convince us, as individuals, of what is and is not true. He called these impulses a system of "Can't Helps": We Can't Help believing them because, to us, they seem so true. "Men to a great extent believe what they want to," Holmes wrote, "although I see in that no basis for a philosophy that tells us what we should want to want."

Holmes was a free man, both in the physical world and in his intellectual world. He was free to think without restraint. He had no need to defer to a "higher power." His thoughts were entirely his own. As Biddle eloquently wrote:

> There could never be reconciliation between the dogmatic mind and the free mind. In spite of efforts to bridge the gap between those who cherish some Being outside their own world because they cannot bear the terror of standing alone, and men like Holmes who find their strength and faith within themselves, the chasm remains, and it is idle to

---

[30] Holmes, "Natural Law," *supra*, 40.

deny its depth. The fanatical believer, who cannot view those who do not agree with him except as evil men, must never be tolerant, for tolerance might open the gates of understanding.[31]

Judge Charles E. Wyzanski, Jr., agreed with most knowledgeable observers that intellectually Holmes was a skeptic, whose "rigorous separation of what he knew from what he did not know was never uttered in arrogance or pride. Indeed he disdained the impetuous defiance of our modern Prometheus, Bertrand Russell. ..."[32] Continuing, Wyzanski wrote:

> Rigorous standards for himself and tolerance of his neighbor were, to be sure, two important articles of his creed. Yet each of these derived from this more basic postulate: although absolute truth, undiminished beauty, unalloyed good are not to be found by man, the never-ending quest for the true, the good, and the beautiful is the activity most satisfying to man.[33]

Holmes's mind was unshackled by the prejudices and intolerance of supposedly eternal principles. His thought was his own. His closest friend on the U.S. Supreme Court, Justice Louis Brandeis, was once asked if he had ever heard Holmes "express a conviction about mankind." Brandeis answered,

---

[31] Biddle, *Justice Holmes, Natural Law, and the Supreme Court*, 49.
[32] Wyzanski, *Whereas*, 40–41.
[33] Ibid., 43–45.

"Holmes had a conviction that man should be free in a large way. He was a great liberator. He was a great originator."[34]

Holmes's skepticism was not grounded in pessimism. Intellectual liberty and tolerance of others' views were a release for Holmes. Freedom of thought brought satisfaction over his long life. He could think of anything, challenge anything, unrestrained by the narrow rules of prejudice and superstition.

Holmes greatly enjoyed life as it was and wrote eloquently of natural beauty. In a March 1, 1923 letter to Harold Laski, he said:

> The tops of the elms begin to thicken with swelling buds — and there is a hint of sunshine today. Brandeis and I felicitate ourselves that the spring is drawing near.[35]

On May 1 of the same year he told Laski of a drive he and his wife took in Washington:

> [O]n the other side of the road by the Potomac basin — lately framed in cherry blossoms at just a picturesque distance was a long bed of tulips — embowered with avenues of trees through which shone the declining sun — while maidens cantered by the side of it and three mockingbirds sang the poetry of the moment. Nature can do some things that man can't quite reproduce.

---

[34] Biddle, *Justice Holmes, Natural Law, and the Supreme Court*, 18.
[35] Howe (ed.), *Holmes–Laski Letters*, I, 485.

Holmes, spring 1928, in a field of flowers near Rock Creek Park, Washington, D.C. (*Courtesy of Historical & Special Collections, Harvard Law School Library. Record ID: olvwork390399*)

[W]hat right have we to feel superior to our brothers because our sense of the beautiful is different? You do like beer or you don't, but how is either better than the other?[36]

John Rawls, the philosopher and political theorist, wrote a book called *A Theory of Justice* that is useful in describing the kind of objective, detached thought that Holmes achieved.[37]

---

[36] *Ibid.*, 692.
[37] Rawls was the James Bryant Conant University Professor, Harvard University. He authored other books on philosophy and justice, all from Harvard.

Rawls constructed his theory of justice based on the hypothetical premise that if people know how a decision of, say, a court will affect them personally they will decide selfishly, in their own interests. Rawls's vehicle for achieving objectivity and personal detachment from decision-making is his notion of a "veil of ignorance."[38] Rawls repeatedly stressed that this device is purely hypothetical. But his two goals are practical: (1) to achieve "equality in the assignment of basic rights and duties;" and (2) to adopt principles for "compensating benefits for everyone, and in particular the least advantaged members of society."[39] These rights and benefits are the kinds that our constitutional Bill of Rights and the 13th, 14th, and 15th Amendments were designed to protect.

Achieving detachment in decision-making by judges is obviously a worthy goal. As we have seen, Holmes thought the notion of "natural law" was groundless. Poles apart was St. Thomas Aquinas, the 13th century monk who, as Rawls pointed out, advocated "the death penalty for heretics on the ground that it is a far graver matter to corrupt the faith, which is the life of the soul, than to counterfeit money which sustains life."[40] Continuing, Rawls said, "It is a matter of dogma that faith is the life of the soul and that the suppression of heresy, that is, departures from ecclesiastical

---

[38] John Rawls, *A Theory of Justice* Rev. Ed. (Cambridge, Massachusetts, 1999), 10–11.
[39] *Ibid.*, 13.
[40] Thomas Aquinas, *Summa Theologica,* II–Q. 11, article 3, as cited in Rawls, *A Theory of Justice,* 189.

authority, is necessary for the safety of souls."[41] "[W]ith Aquinas and the Protestant Reformers the grounds of intolerance are themselves a matter of faith."[42] Positive laws, in contrast, "are directives addressed to rational persons for their guidance. ..."[43] Rawls's construct of the "veil of ignorance" may be seen as a useful mental tool for attaining objectivity. As will be seen, Holmes rigorously demanded from himself personal detachment in decision-making. He refused to succumb to the temptation of injecting his personal views into his judicial opinions.

Thus, we see how Oliver Wendell Holmes was "defining the law" during his young scholarly years and well beyond. In 1880–1881, the fruits of his labor were those Lowell Lectures — in book form Holmes's "definition" of *The Common Law*. By 1918 he was defining — and rejecting — "natural law."

---

[41] *Ibid.*, Rawls, *A Theory of Justice*, 189.
[42] *Ibid.*, 190.
[43] *Ibid.*, 210.

One of two large rooms in the Library of Congress, upstairs on "Mahogany Row" facing the U.S. Capitol, and filled with a substantial portion of Justice Holmes's eclectic, prolific, and treasured book collection from both Beverly Farms and his Washington residence at 1720 Eye Street.
(*Courtesy of Eric Frazier, Holmes Collection, Rare Books and Special Collections, Library of Congress*)

6

ERUDITION

"The prevalence of reason."

CORRESPONDENCE BETWEEN Holmes and friends opens a window into his mind. His letters provide a glimpse of the world of ideas in which he lived. Holmes wrote about a wide range of subjects: the books he read, the art he saw and even purchased, trips he took, people he visited, conversations he had, jokes he had heard, religion, philosophy, and numerous other topics. It is likely that solitary writing stimulated his mind, as conversations with friends would do.

Francis Biddle wrote that Holmes was "an immense reader in several languages, catholic in his taste and wide in his range."[1] The languages included French, German, Latin, and Greek. He kept a black notebook in which he listed the books he had read each year, then gave the list to his clerk for that year. When Biddle clerked for Holmes in 1910, Holmes had read forty-nine books. In 1934, two years after he retired from the Court — one year before he died — the list showed he had read 116 books that year since he had no court work to do.

Holmes told Biddle that when he eventually retired "he had to fill in gaps in his reading, for when he arrived at the

---

[1] Biddle, *Justice Holmes, Natural Law, and the Supreme Court*, 5.

A shelf of Justice Holmes's books includes Emerson's and Holmes Sr.'s titles.
(*Courtesy of Eric Frazier, Holmes Collection, Rare Books and Special Collections, Library of Congress*)

Pearly Gates the first question St. Peter would ask him was whether he had read *The Decline and Fall*."[2]

Holmes's erudition is reflected in the books he read and discussed in hundreds of letters to friends. The scope of his reading and subjects encompassed in a lifetime of reading are remarkably broad. Subjects include science, philosophy, history, art, and fiction. Any discussion can do only partial justice to his reading without becoming voluminous. We discuss a thin slice of the whole loaf. Even this much gives a hint of the eclectic nature of his reading.

Thomas Hobbes, the 16th-and 17th-century philosopher, author of *Leviathan* and *Human Nature*, gave Holmes great joy. He wrote, "Every other sentence is an epigram that one

---

[2] *Ibid.*, 6.

wants to save for quotation in a dissent."[3] He was lukewarm on John Galsworthy's novel *In Chancery*. He thought the "reminiscences of Mrs. Humphrey Ward gloriously amusing," she "measures herself against G. Eliot," but "really belonged to that amiable gentleman of whom Oida and Mrs. Oliphant are the leaders."[4] Holmes thought the novel *My Antonia* by Willa Cather was a "really great novel … turning the life of early settlers on the prairie (in our time) so hard, so squalid into a noble poem."[5]

It seems fitting that Holmes's book collection in the Library of Congress looks out upon the U.S. Capitol Dome. Holmes was wounded three times in serving the Union during the Civil War. Justice Holmes served on the U.S. Supreme Court for thirty years.
(*Courtesy of Eric Frazier, Holmes Collection, Rare Books and Special Collections, Library of Congress*)

---

[3] Howe (ed.), *Holmes-Laski Letters*, I, 258.
[4] *Ibid.*, 259.
[5] *Ibid.*, II, 1269.

First page of a long alphabetical list, Holmes's book collection, entitled "Estate of Justice Holmes: The Library: Beverly Farms, Massachusetts."
(*Courtesy of Eric Frazier, Holmes Collection, Rare Books and Special Collections, Library of Congress*)

He enjoyed Trollope's *Orley Farm*. Cardinal J. H. Newman's *Apologia* and the *Grammar of Assent* were "exquisite."[6] In 1921 he said [G. W.] Hegel "couldn't make me believe that a syllogism could wag its tail," mentioning Hegel's *Logic*. This remained the view he had expressed forty years earlier in *The Common Law*: "The life of the law has not been logic; it has been experience."[7]

---

[6] *Ibid.*, I, 407.
[7] Holmes, *The Common Law*, 1.

ERUDITION

Holmes wrote Laski on April 6, 1920:

> Truth is the unanimous consent to a system of propositions. It is an ideal and as such postulates itself as a thing to be attained, but like other good ideals it is unattainable and therefore may be called absurd. Some ideals, like morality, a system of specific conduct for every situation, would be detestable if attained and therefore the postulate must be conditioned — that it is a thing to be striven for on the tacit understanding that it will not be reached.

Holmes closed his letter with the statement, "I must go in 5 minutes to a conference of the JJ [justices] and therefore run down with a bump."[8]

In a single letter to Laski on August 8, 1924, Holmes wrote, "I delight" in Bernoulli's work "apropos of Newton's solution." Montaigne seemed "more than companionable," and "had profound philosophic insights and covers more ground than Pascal … Macaulay does not hit me hard," but "he made an early and illuminating application of Bentham in the penal code for India … and wrote some good poems in spite of M. Arnold …" He said, "I have been taken up with Thucydides." "[J]ust as I hate to read about our civil war I don't like to read much of the blunders and misfortunes of those one loves of 2,000 years ago … I reflect with satisfaction that while that was going on Socrates was firing away and that the political fall of Athens was the beginning of her leadership in philosophy. I read books 1 and 2 and 7 in the Greek, and the rest, not quite finished in the translation with only an

---

[8] Howe (ed.), *Holmes-Laski Letters*, I, 258–259.

occasional eye to the original." He closed saying, "I want to post this this morning" and "The machine is here."⁹

Holmes wrote this letter, and countless others, from Beverly Farms while the Supreme Court was in recess. There he could read, reflect, and write at length.

Another random sample is a letter from Holmes to Laski on June 15, 1924, again sent from Beverly Farms. Holmes discussed the novelist Marcel Proust and William Hazlitt, the British essayist. He was reading *Persae* by Aeschylus, the Greek writer; *Tertium Organum* by Ouspensky; and the German philosopher Oswald Spengler's *Der Untergang des Abendlandes*, noting that "in these last years German and Greek come a little easier to me than they did." Holmes said, "When the Grand Duke [Alexis of Russia] was in Boston before [Laski] was born," he and Holmes "had some philosophic discourse and more wine." He continued, "I have recurred to the unfinished *Causeries* of [Charles Augustin] Saint-Beuve, the French literary critic and writer." He was returning to Henri Bergson, the French philosopher. He closed this letter, asking "Don't you think that these square pointed pens are stinking?"¹⁰

Holmes continued to discuss in letters a wide range of subjects through the 1920's. He thought "clericalism" was "childish." He said "my conviction is only faith in the prevalence of reason in the long run … but I am well aware

---

⁹ *Ibid.*, 644–645.
¹⁰ *Ibid.*, 624–625.

how long reason may be kept under by what man wants to believe. I do despise the Will to Believe."[11]

Holmes often said he agreed with the 17th century philosopher Baruch Spinoza who thought "God is nature," and "there is nothing ultimately mysterious in the world; there are no inscrutable deities making arbitrary decisions, ... in short, that there is nothing that cannot be known, even if we do not necessarily know everything."[12] Holmes had read Spinoza's *Ethics*, among other works, and said Spinoza "sees the world as I do." John Dewey, the U.S. philosopher and educator, was "another man who sees the world somewhat as I do."[13]

Holmes carried on a lively correspondence with many other friends, including Sir Frederick Pollock, Felix Frankfurter, Learned Hand, and many of his former law clerks. His letters reveal more than his erudition. They also demonstrate his unfailing warmth and kindness.

An example is his correspondence with the Irish priest, Canon Patrick Augustine Sheehan. The two men were poles apart in their beliefs. But their letters reflect mutual respect and friendliness. In February 1904, Holmes wrote Sheehan, "I simply want to tell you more emphatically than before now that I have finished your book [and] that I owe you my admiration and thanks."[14]

---

[11] *Ibid.*, II, 1134.
[12] Matthew Stewart, *The Courtier and the Heretic: Leibniz, Spinoza, and the Fate of God in the Modern World* (New Haven, 2006), 158–159.
[13] Howe (ed.), *Holmes-Laski Letters*, II, 1135, February 22, 1929.
[14] David H. Burton (ed.), *Holmes-Sheehan Correspondence: Letters of Justice Oliver Wendell Holmes, Jr. and Canon Patrick Augustine Sheehan* Rev. Ed. (New York, 1993), 21.

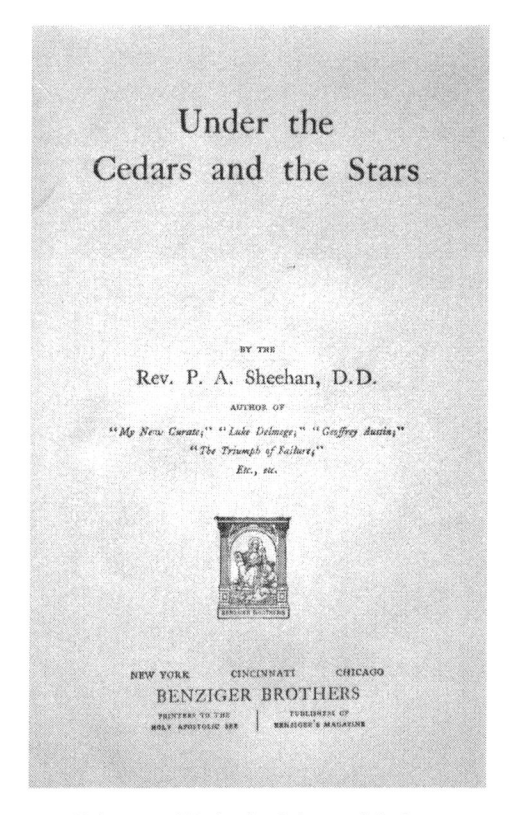

Title page of *Under the Cedars and the Stars*
by Canon Patrick Augustus Sheehan (1852–1913).
(Courtesy of Eric Frazier, Holmes Collection, Rare Books and Special Collections, Library of Congress)

On August 26, 1908, Holmes wrote Sheehan from Beverly Farms which he described as "a little place near the sea where we have our summer outfit."[15] He said, "I have bought a two-third interest in the place ... to avoid the risk of being turned out and rather expect to buy the other one-third before long."[16] Holmes said, "I wish I could see you in it."[17]

---

[15] *Ibid.*, 35.
[16] *Ibid.*

Holmes again wrote Sheehan from Beverly Farms on July 5, 1912, saying "...I want to know how you are, and what new expression your beautiful spirit is finding." He said, "What a refuge your religion is from the terrors of the universe. I could not believe it except by a total collapse — but it must be a joy and warm up the interstellar spaces."[18]

Holmes's faith in the power of reason extended to his views of the economy. Holmes was an economic conservative. For instance, he had no use for the Sherman antitrust law. After hearing an argument in an antitrust case, he walked from court with John W. Davis, then Solicitor General, who had argued for the government. "Mr. Solicitor," asked Holmes, "how many of these economic policy cases have you got?" "Quite a basketful," Davis answered. "Well," said Holmes, "bring 'em on and we'll decide 'em. Of course I know, and every other sensible man knows, that the Sherman law is damned nonsense, but if my country wants to go to hell I am here to help it."[19]

It is interesting to compare the legal thought of Holmes with that of other contemporaries. For instance, in voiding the Agricultural Adjustment Act, an important piece of FDR's New Deal legislation, Justice Owen J. Roberts, writing for the majority in the 1936 case *U.S. v. Butler*,[20] said that to judge the constitutionality of an act of Congress all that was necessary was "to lay the article of the Constitution which is invoked

---

[17] *Ibid.*
[18] *Ibid.*, 65.
[19] Biddle, *Justice Holmes, Natural Law, and the Supreme Court*, 9.
[20] 297 U.S. 1 (1936).

beside the statute which is challenged and to decide whether the latter squares with the former."

Bound catalogue of Holmes's Beverly Farms books.
(*Courtesy of Eric Frazier, Holmes Collection, Rare Books and Special Collections, Library of Congress*)

In contrast, Holmes thought the Constitutional provisions are "not mathematical formulas having their essence in the form; [but] organic living institutions transplanted from English soil. Their significance is vital not formal; it is to be gathered not simply by taking the words of a dictionary, but by considering their origin and their line of growth."[21]

Holmes's letters to his British friends Harold Laski and Sir Frederick Pollock are contained in two volumes each, edited by Mark DeWolfe Howe, a Harvard Law School professor. Howe has done heroic work in leaving to posterity a trove of

---

[21] Biddle, *Justice Holmes, Natural Law, and the Supreme Court*, 75.

Holmes's ideas expressed in nearly indecipherable handwriting. Howe's work of "translation," tedious as it must have been to do it, is a gift. Howe also wrote two volumes of a biography of Holmes before his untimely death. He had intended to write additional works. Howe's scholarship was probably the most reliable work done on Holmes. He relied on facts and exhaustive research. He never speculated or offered unprovable impressions. If Howe said it, you can take it to the bank.

Justice Oliver Wendell Holmes, c. 1924.
(*Courtesy of Library of Congress*)

7

STYLE OF HOLMES'S OPINIONS

"The prevalence of reason."

HOLMES WAS ALWAYS gentlemanly in expressing his views. In his legal opinions he never personally attacked those who disagreed with him. This is a large statement when seen in the light of the savage and *ad hominem* verbal assaults on differing views that are all too common on today's Supreme Court. For instance, in a recent book, *The Case Against the Supreme Court*, the author, a noted constitutional scholar, writes, "… I believe that the increasing use of sarcasm and even ridicule in judicial opinions is undesirable. No justice in Supreme Court history has consistently written with the sarcasm of Justice [Antonin] Scalia."[1] Continuing, the author wrote:

> Examples of this abound. In dissenting opinions, he describes the majority's approaches as "nothing short of ludicrous" and "beyond absurd," "entirely irrational" and not "pass[ing] the most gullible scrutiny." He has declared that a majority opinion was "nothing short of

---

[1] We note that Justice Scalia recently passed away, after Erwin Chemerinsky's comments were written.

preposterous" and that it had "no foundation in American law and barely pretends to."[2]

Scalia said that "Today's tale ... is so transparently false that professing to believe it demeans this institution," and "the Court makes itself the obfuscator of last result."[3]

Another recent example of provocative language by Justice Scalia was recounted in a December 3, 2015 article by Judge Richard A. Posner and law professor Eric J. Segall, entitled "Scalia's Majoritarian Theocracy."[4] Commenting on the June 2015 case *Obergefell v. Hodges*, which held that the Constitution protects the right to same-sex marriage, the article says that Justice Scalia "vented even more than his usual anger over this decision." Another writer notes that the opinion in *Obergefell* by Justice Anthony Kennedy "provoked Justice Scalia to paroxysms of outrage in dissent."[5] Further, the Posner and Segall article reports: "In a recent speech to law students at Georgetown, he argued that there is no

---

[2] Erwin Chemerinsky, *The Case Against the Supreme Court* (New York, 2014), 323–324. Erwin Chemerinsky is the former founding dean and Distinguished Professor of Law, and Raymond Pryke Professor of First Amendment Law at the University of California, Irvine School of Law. Currently he is dean at the University of California, Berkeley School of Law. His areas of expertise are constitutional law, federal practice, civil rights, civil liberties, and appellate litigation. He has argued several cases at the Supreme Court.

[3] *Ibid.*, 324.

[4] Richard A. Posner and Eric J. Segall, "Scalia's Majoritarian Theocracy," *The New York Times*, December 3, 2015, p. A35.

[5] Tobias Barrington Wolff, "The Three Voices of Obergefell," *Los Angeles Lawyer*, December 2015, p. 31.

principled basis for distinguishing child molesters from homosexuals, since both are minorities and, further, that the protection of minorities should be the responsibility of legislators, not courts. After all, he remarked sarcastically, child molesters are also a 'deserving minority,' and added, 'nobody loves them.'"[6]

Dissenting in a 2016 decision holding that juveniles may not constitutionally be imprisoned for life without parole, Scalia again wrote with characteristic acerbity. He said, "[I]n Godfather fashion, the majority makes an offer they can't refuse: Avoid all the impossible nonsense we have prescribed by simply 'permitting juvenile homicide offenders to be considered for parole' … Mission accomplished."[7]

Reading such goading, provocative language, we wonder what the author thought he was accomplishing by using it. In his own words during a television interview, Justice Scalia explained, "I attack ideas, I don't attack people. And some very good people have some very bad ideas. And if you can't separate the two, you gotta get another day job." After a few seconds, he proudly added that he was a "shin kicker." Do his explanations describe attacking ideas, or attacking "shins" *ad hominem*, or both?[8]

In marked contrast, Holmes's opinions, speeches, letters, and conversation were always polite and gentlemanly. He undoubtedly understood that polite language was more

---

[6] Posner and Segall, "Scalia's Majoritarian Theocracy," p. A35.
[7] As of December 20, 2016: *Obergefell v. Hodges*, 135 S. Ct. 2584, 192 L. Ed. 2nd 609, 83 U.S.L.W. 4592 (2015).
[8] Justice Scalia's remarks aired on a year 2016 retrospective, "CBS News Sunday Morning," January 1, 2017.

convincing than words of denunciation. But more than that, civility was in Holmes's nature.

Holmes was also a legal pragmatist. He thought legal rights were the rights that were enforceable. His view of enforceability was based entirely on what actually happens. As we have seen, Holmes wrote in *The Common Law* that, "The life of the law has not been logic: it has been experience." A given statute or rule may be logical or illogical, good or bad, but it is nothing more than words if it cannot be enforced. Holmes was describing the world he encountered, not one he wished would exist.

Oliver Wendell Holmes, Jr., left.
Harris & Ewing, photographer. United States, 1932 [or 1933].
(*Courtesy of Library of Congress*)

For Holmes the Constitution was adopted to be a practical, useful instrument. He would not agree with the judges and theorists who claim that the meaning of the Constitution does not evolve, that only the "original intent" of the framers may be considered in construing its meaning. Indeed, Justice Scalia was a leading champion of "original intent." In contrast, Holmes said it is "revolting to have no better reason for a rule of law than that it was laid down in the time of Henry IV. It is still more revolting if the grounds upon which it was laid down have vanished long since, and the rule simply persists from blind imitation of the past."[9]

---

[9] *See* Howe, *Justice Oliver Wendell Holmes,* I, *The Shaping Years,* vii; Holmes, "The Path of the Law," 457, 469.

Massachusetts Supreme Judicial Court, John Adams Courthouse, Boston.

8

Massachusetts Supreme Judicial Court

"Free competition is worth more to society than it costs."

On January 3, 1883, Holmes took his seat as the youngest among seven judges on the Massachusetts Supreme Judicial Court, where he would serve until the end of 1902. Biographer Liva Baker captures the significance:

> It was what Holmes had been practicing for all his life. All those threads that often had seemed irrelevant to the pattern of his life were coming together. Family, old and established, had given him a liberating sense of security that allowed him to challenge tradition. Soldiering had taught him about determination and showed him what courage meant at the same time it had demanded both from him. As a student at Harvard Law School he had mastered the "ragbag of details" that made up the law in mid-nineteenth century. As a young lawyer he had experienced the law office and the courtroom, then reinterpreted what the masters said about the law. As a slightly older lawyer, he had had the audacity to advance his original ideas about the law. It remained only for him to decide the law.[1]

---

[1] Baker, *The Justice from Beacon Hill*, 269–270.

Mahogany stand-up desk used by Massachusetts Supreme Court Justice Charles Jackson and his grandson, Chief Justice of the Massachusetts Supreme Judicial Court, Oliver Wendell Holmes, Jr. About his stand-up desk, Holmes once joked, "Nothing conduces to brevity of expression like a weakness in the knees."
(*Courtesy of Historical & Special Collections, Harvard Law School Library.*
Record ID: olvwork416272)

In a handful of opinions while serving on the Massachusetts Supreme Judicial Court, Holmes expressed views on both law and life that he would hone and sharpen for the rest of his long career and life.

Vegelahn v. Guntner[2] enjoined current or future employees from patrolling on the sidewalk or street in front of a business. The majority opinion held this conduct was a means of "intimidation" and "an unlawful interference with the

---

[2] 167 Massachusetts 92 (1896).

rights of both employer and of employed." Moreover, the court believed the patrols "also may be a moral intimidation which is illegal." The opinion did not define the meaning of "moral intimidation."

Holmes dissented. He found that peaceful patrols were nothing more than *"free competition* [which] is worth more to society than it costs, and that on this ground the infliction of the damage is privileged." Indeed, said Holmes, "the policy of allowing free competition justifies the intentional inflicting of temporal damage ... as an instrumentality in reaching the end of victory in the battle of trade."[3]

The idea of life as a battle — probably a remnant of his Civil War experience — was central to Holmes's thought. Competition between interests large and small, employer and employee, is perfectly lawful, thought Holmes, and cannot be enjoined. Holmes expressed his view of law and life:

> One of the internal conflicts of which life is made up is that between the effort of every man to get the most he can for his services and that of society disguised under the name of capital, for the least possible return. Combination [of labor] on the one hand is patent and powerful. Combination [of employers] on the other is the necessary counterpart, if the battle is to be carried off in a fair and equal way.

This dissent foreshadowed Holmes's dissent in a later Sherman Act antitrust decision by the U. S. Supreme Court in the case of *Northern Securities Co. v. United States,*[4] in which

---

[3] *Ibid.,* 92, emphasis added.
[4] 193 U.S. 197 (1904).

the Court's majority affirmed a decree ordering that a "monopoly" between two railroads be broken up. This case is more fully discussed below.[5]

Holmes's and Fanny's first house [1883–1889, at "9 Orchard St." (now 9 Chestnut St.)]. Justice Holmes walked from here to the MSJC courthouse a few blocks away.
(*Courtesy of Leslie and Alastair Adam*)

Four years later, Holmes, now Chief Justice of the Massachusetts Supreme Judicial Court, joined the battle again in *Plant v. Woods*,[6] involving a clash between two labor unions. The defendant union threatened strikes and boycotts, and implied that the employer "should fear trouble" if it continued to employ members of the plaintiff union. The majority thought the defendant's conduct was intended to strike for a closed shop, to obtain an agreement from employers that they would hire only members of the

---

[5] *See also,* Charles Oscar Gregory, *Labor and the Law* (New York, 1946), 60: *Vegelahn* "is chiefly important because of the challenging dissent by Judge Holmes."
[6] 176 Massachusetts 492 (1900).

defendant union. The court held that those threats were not legitimate and were "intolerable and inconsistent with the spirit of our laws."[7]

Dissenting again, Holmes said, "The difference between my Brethren and me seems to be a difference of degree, ... whether the purpose in this case of the threatened boycotts and strikes was such as to justify the threats." He viewed the strike as a lawful instrument in "the universal struggle of life." As he had in *Vegelahn*, he upheld peaceful competition between conflicting forces.

---

[7] *Ibid.*, 502.

The Taft Court visits the White House.
(Washington, DC): National Photo, October 4, 1921.
(*Courtesy of The Lawbook Exchange, Ltd.*)

9

UNITED STATES SUPREME COURT

"The Sherman Act says nothing about competition."

IN 1902, President Theodore Roosevelt appointed his acquaintance Holmes to the United States Supreme Court. Holmes was 61, an age at which many people are retired. Yet he served for 30 years, until 1932.

It didn't take long for a conflict to arise between Holmes and the mercurial President. Two years after his appointment Holmes faced a monumental issue, the impact of the 1890 Sherman Act on competition among large interests. In *Northern Securities Co. v. United States*, a 5-4 majority held that under the Act, Northern Securities Co., a trust holding stock in two rival railroads, was a combination in restraint of trade in violation of the Act. The Court enjoined Northern Securities from acquiring more stock and from voting the stock it held.

Holmes dissented. He had by now hit his stride as a mature judicial writer. Typically, in dissent he began with an arresting phrase. His dissent began: "Great cases, like hard cases, make bad law."[1] He explained:

---

[1] *Northern Securities Co v. U.S. [supra]*, 400–401.

For great cases are called great not by reason of their real importance in shaping the law of the future but because of some accident of immediate overwhelming interest which appeals to the feelings and distorts the judgment. These immediate interests exercise a kind of hydraulic pressure which makes what previously was clear seem doubtful, and before which even well-settled principles of law will bend. What we have to do in this case is to find the meaning of some not very difficult words ....[2]

Holmes quickly stated the issue in the case:

The question to be decided is whether, under the [Act] ... it is unlawful, at any stage of the process, if several men unite to form a corporation for the purpose of buying more than half the stock of two competing railroad companies with the single intent of ending competition between the companies.[3]

Holmes strictly construed the words of Congress in creating the Act. He pointed out that section one says "*every* contract in restraint of trade is a crime."[4] He emphasized that under this language, "Size has nothing to do with the matter. A monopoly of 'any part' of commerce among the states is unlawful."[5] Continuing, Holmes said:

---

[2] *Ibid.,* 401.
[3] *Ibid.*
[4] *Ibid.,* 406 (emphasis added).
[5] *Ibid.,* 407.

Justices Oliver Wendell Holmes, Jr. and Louis Dembitz Brandeis served together on the U.S. Supreme Court from 1916–1932, including the Taft Court (1921–1930). (*Courtesy of Historical & Special Collections, Harvard Law School Library. Record ID: olvwork370664*)

There is a natural feeling that somehow or other the statute meant to strike at combinations great enough to cause just anxiety on the part of those who love their country more than money, while it viewed the little ones as I have supposed them with just indifference. This notion, it may be said, somehow breathes from the pores of the act, although it seems to be contradicted in every way by the words in detail.[6]

---

[6] *Ibid.*

Holmes emphasized that the law *"says nothing about competition."* He tested his point that the Act equally applies to companies that are "little ones." He said, "To see whether I am wrong ... then a partnership between two stage drivers who had been competitors in driving across a state line, or two merchants once engaged in rival commerce among the states, whether made after or before the act, if now continued, is a crime ...."[7]

Holmes was "happy to know that only a minority of my brethren adopt an interpretation of the law which, in my opinion would ... disintegrate society so far as it could into individual atoms."[8] Holmes thought that if Congress did have such an intent, he would see "calling such a law a regulation of commerce [for jurisdictional purposes] as a mere pretense," which would raise serious constitutional issues. But Holmes was "deeply persuaded that [Congress] has not tried."[9] Holmes closed his dissent, stating, "I am authorized to say the Chief Justice, Mr. Justice White, and Mr. Justice Peckham concur in this result."[10]

Theodore Roosevelt was sorely disappointed by Justice Holmes's dissent. "I could carve out of a banana a judge with more backbone than that," the president reportedly quipped.[11]

Holmes shared contempt for the 1890 Sherman Antitrust Act with his old Boston Brahmin friend Richard Olney. Back in 1895, after Attorney General Olney's failed prosecution of

---

[7] *Ibid.*, 410.
[8] *Ibid.*, 411.
[9] *Ibid.*
[10] *Ibid.*
[11] Catherine Drinker Bowen, *Yankee from Olympus* (Boston, 1944), 370.

E.C. Knight Co., Olney had said he never thought the Sherman Act was any good and would never use it again.[12]

Though not widely noticed, Holmes's deferential and literal construction of Congress's words in the Sherman Act, his refusal to construe the law broadly, thus avoiding a constitutional collision, was the beginning of his doctrine of judicial restraint. Holmes's dissent in *Northern Securities* focused on Congress's intent by construing the *whole* of one of its statutes. Holmes's dissent also foreshadowed Chief Justice John Roberts's majority opinion in the 2015 case *King v. Burwell*, similarly construing the *whole* statute to determine the intent of Congress in its 2010 healthcare legislation, the Affordable Care Act.

---

[12] Allan Nevins, *Study in Power: John D. Rockefeller* (New York, 1953), II, 362.

Oliver Wendell Holmes, Jr., in judicial robes (1903).
(Courtesy of Library of Congress)

10

The Lochner Era and Judicial Restraint

"The 14th Amendment does not enact Mr. Herbert Spencer's Social Statics."

THE LEGAL WORLD of the mid-to-late 19th and early 20th centuries saw a struggle over the meaning and scope of the Reconstruction Amendments, also called the "Civil War Amendments": the 13th abolishing slavery; the 14th granting certain civil rights; and the 15th guaranteeing the right to vote. A major issue involved the power of government to regulate commercial interests under the due process clause of the 14th Amendment, which provides that no state shall "deprive any person of life, liberty, or property, without due process of law." On one side of the struggle was the *laissez faire* view of the entrepreneurial class which held that government had no business interfering with the economy. On the other side, government was beginning to see that an unregulated private economy would run roughshod over legitimate interests of less powerful citizens of the nation. The struggle would produce tectonic changes in the ways America governed itself.

The early decisions of the Supreme Court reflected a permissive view of government's regulatory power. Seven years after the Civil War, in the *Slaughterhouse Cases,*[1] the Court held that a Louisiana law chartering a corporation and giving it the exclusive right to operate a slaughterhouse in New Orleans did not violate the property rights of other New Orleans butchers who wanted to compete in that market.

In 1877, the Court in *Munn v. Illinois*[2] held that an Illinois law fixing maximum prices that could be charged for storage of grain did not deny warehouse operators property rights. Determination of the reasonableness of the prices, the court said, could have reasonably been made by the legislature, not the courts. The next year, in *Davidson v. New Orleans,*[3] the Court upheld a Louisiana statute providing for a special assessment against property for drainage purposes.

Between 1878 and 1900, as the personnel of the Court changed, it gradually narrowed government's right to regulate the economy under both the due process and equal protection clauses of the 14th Amendment, and broadened its own power to, in effect, second-guess legislatures.

The Court's 1890 decision in *Chicago, Milwaukee, and Saint Paul R.R. v. Minnesota*[4] is an example. The Court held that Minnesota's rate commission had interfered with the property rights of railroads by failing to provide for judicial review of rates set by the commission. Rate setting, the Court held, was "eminently a question for judicial investigation, requiring due process of law for its determination." A dissent

---

[1] *Butchers' Benevolent Association of New Orleans v. Crescent City Live-Stock Landing & Slaughterhouse Co.*, 83 U.S. (16 Wall.) 36 (1873).
[2] 94 U.S. 113 (1877).
[3] 96 U.S. 97 (1878).
[4] 134 U.S. 418 (1890).

by one justice sensibly argued that the fairness of rates was a "legislative question, not a judicial one."

In 1894, Justice David Josiah Brewer authored the majority opinion in *Reagan v. Farmer's Loan and Trust*[5] stating that "the acquisition, possession and enjoyment of property" are sacred pursuits "which human government cannot forbid and which it cannot destroy."[6] In fact, wrote Brewer, there is a due process right to a "fair return" for corporations.[7]

Such extreme *laissez faire* decisions continued to roll out of the Supreme Court. In 1895, *Pollock v. Farmer's Loan and Trust Co.*[8] held that the federal income tax was unconstitutional. Over the years, the Court continued to "discover" other constitutional rights to remain wealthy.[9] It may fairly be said that such decisions were made by judges empowering themselves to act as legislators in judicial robes. They regarded the Constitution as an empty vessel into which they could pour their personal views.

The Court went even further in 1898. In *Smyth v. Ames*,[10] the Court prescribed the exact formula for calculating the "reasonableness of rates" a corporation could charge for maintaining a highway.[11]

---

[5] 154 U.S. 362 (1894).
[6] *Ibid.*, 412.
[7] *Ibid.*, 399.
[8] 157 U.S. 429 (1895), 601, 604.
[9] Burns, *Packing the Court*, 110–111.
[10] 169 U.S. 466, 546 (1898).
[11] *See also* Franklin H. Cook, "History of Rate Determination under Due Process Clauses," *University of Chicago Law Review* 11 (1944), 297; Leon

Joseph Lochner in the yard behind his bakery with his wife, a neighborhood child, his son, and three bakery employees.
(*Photo credit: Mrs. John J. Brady*)

The critical issue involved in these cases was the constitutional allocation of powers between the legislative and judicial branches of government. In particular, the question was, what is the proper role of the judiciary in reviewing the constitutionality of laws?

Looking back, the decisions in cases such as *Chicago, Milwaukee, and St. Paul R.R., Reagan,* and *Smyth* are startling. The idea that courts would assume the authority to set rates charged by railroads and companies maintaining roads, and declare a "right" to a fair profit, are unimaginable in light of today's due process standards.

Thus, when Holmes took his seat on the court in 1902, the stage was set. Some two years later, Holmes had his first

---

Jourolmon, Jr., "The Life and Death of Smyth v. Ames," *Tennessee Law Review* 18 (1943–1945), 347, 663, 756.

chance to join the battle. He did so in one of the most celebrated dissents in America's judicial history.

In *Lochner v. New York*,[12] the Supreme Court reversed the misdemeanor conviction of the owner of a bakery for violating a New York labor and public health law. The statute forbade an employer from allowing an employee to work more than sixty hours a week. Such a statute, judged by today's standards, seems remarkably unobjectionable. But in 1905, the law was greeted with a barrage of opposition on the Supreme Court.

Justice Rufus W. Peckham wrote the majority opinion. According to one writer, Holmes "once said the major premise of Peckham's jurisprudence was 'God Damn it' ...."[13] Peckham and Justice Brewer, who joined the majority opinion, "believed in individual *natural rights* to liberty and property."[14] As it had done routinely in the decisions discussed above, the Court's majority opinion denounced the law as a violation of the "liberty clause" of the 14th Amendment. The Court declared that the law "necessarily interferes with the right of contract between the employer and employees concerning the number of hours in which the latter may labor in the bakery of the employer. The general *right to make a contract* in relation to his business is part of the *liberty of the individual* protected by the 14th Amendment of the Federal Constitution."[15] The New York law, said the

---

[12] 198 U.S. 45 (1905).
[13] Evan Tsen Lee, *Judicial Restraint in America: How the Ageless Wisdom of the Supreme Court Was Invented* (New York, 2011), 26.
[14] *Ibid.*, emphasis added.
[15] *Ibid.*, 53, emphasis added.

majority, "seriously limits the right to labor or the right of contract in regard to their means of livelihood...."[16]

This "right" of an employee to work more than sixty hours a week is an elusive one. This holding simply injects into the 14th Amendment the justices' personal views of what the constitutional language would provide if the justices were drafting it, thus creating a substantive rule of law.

In a statement that appears defensive, the Court said, "This is not a question of substituting the judgment of the court for that of the legislature."[17] Then the Court substituted its judgment for that of the legislature: "There is, in our judgment, no reasonable foundation for holding this [law] to be necessary or appropriate as a health law to safeguard the public health, or the health of the individuals who are following the trade of a baker."[18]

The Court even questioned the "motive" of the legislature: "When assertions such as we have adverted to become necessary in order to give, if possible, a plausible foundation for the contention that the law is a 'health law,' it gives rise to at least a *suspicion that there was some other motive* dominating the legislature than the purpose to subserve the public health or welfare."[19] The Court did not say what it thought the legislature's "other motive" might have been. Nor did the Court say what business the judiciary has in determining the "motives" of legislators. Further, the Court expressed its fear that, "This interference on the part of the legislatures of the

---

[16] *Ibid.,* 54.
[17] *Ibid.,* 56–57.
[18] *Ibid.,* 58.
[19] *Ibid.,* 62–63, emphasis added.

several states with the ordinary trades and occupations of the people seems to be on the increase."[20] Here was a full-blown decision based on the majority's free-market ideology.

After twenty pages of denunciations of governmental "interference" with "occupations of the people," the Court held that the New York law was unconstitutional and reversed the decisions of the New York state courts upholding the law.

This practice — invalidating legislation that the justices thought conflicted with their own free-market ideologies — became known as "Lochnerizing" a case.[21]

Following Peckham's lengthy opinion, Holmes dissented in three paragraphs. The power and simple eloquence of his dissent would become so widely admired and so persuasive in later years that it would brand as the "Lochner era" decades of Supreme Court decisions overturning state and federal laws based on the ideological biases of the justices. Holmes's dissent articulated a principle that would become known as judicial restraint, the idea that courts should restrain themselves from deciding cases by substituting their views of the *wisdom* of statutes for those of legislatures. Holmes was the first Supreme Court justice to establish the principle.[22] The concept is a separation-of-powers principle lying at the heart of federalism in America's system of government. It recognizes the deference to legislative judgments that courts

---

[20] *Ibid.*, 63.
[21] Gunther, *Learned Hand*, 118.
[22] *See* Posner (ed.), *The Essential Holmes*, xii; Lee, *Judicial Restraint in America*, 54 (Holmes "became the first Supreme Court justice to be identified with" judicial self-restraint).

must require of themselves if democracy is to function as the Constitution envisions.

Holmes's first paragraph was a one-sentence apology: "I regret sincerely that I am unable to agree with the judgment in this case, and that I think it my duty to express my dissent."[23]

Then came the words that today still define the proper role of appellate courts in construing the Constitution.

> This case is decided upon an economic theory which a large part of the country does not entertain. If it were a question whether I agreed with that theory, I should desire to study it further and long before making up my mind. But I do not conceive that to be my duty, because I strongly believe that my agreement or disagreement has nothing to do with *the right of the majority to embody their opinions in law*. It is settled by various decisions of this court that state constitutions and state laws may regulate life in many ways *which we as legislators might think as injudicious, or if you like as tyrannical,* as this, and which, equally with this, interfere with the liberty to contract.[24]

Holmes illustrated his point with familiar examples:

> Sunday laws and usury laws are ancient examples. A more modern one is the prohibition of lotteries. The liberty of the citizen to do as he likes so long as he does not interfere with the liberty of others to do the same, which has been a shibboleth for some well-known writers, is interfered with by school laws, by the Post office, by every state or municipal

---

[23] *Lochner v. New York, supra,* 75–76.
[24] *Ibid.*, emphasis added.

institution which takes his money for purposes thought desirable, whether he likes it or not. *The 14th Amendment does not enact Mr. Herbert Spencer's Social Statics.*[25]

Continuing, Holmes offered his views of the role of the Constitution:

> Some ... laws embody convictions or prejudices which judges are likely to share. Some may not. *But a Constitution is not intended to embody a particular economic theory,* whether of paternalism and the organic relation of the citizen to the state or of *laissez faire*. It is made for people of *fundamentally differing views,* and the accident of our finding certain opinions natural and familiar, or novel, and even shocking, ought not to conclude our judgment upon the question whether statutes embodying them conflict with the Constitution of the United States.[26]

Holmes finished by explaining his view of the meaning of the term "liberty" in the 14th Amendment's protection of "life, liberty, or property."

> *General propositions do not decide concrete cases. The decision will depend on a judgment or intuition more subtle than any articulate major premise.* But I think that the proposition just stated, if it is accepted, will carry us far toward the end. ... *I think the word "liberty" is perverted when it is held to prevent the natural outcome of a dominant opinion,* unless it can be said that a rational and fair man

---

[25] *Ibid.*, emphasis added.
[26] *Ibid.*, emphasis added.

necessarily would admit that the statute proposed would infringe fundamental principles as they have been understood by the traditions of our people and the law. It does not need research to show that no such sweeping condemnation can be passed upon the statute before us. A reasonable man might think it a proper measure on the score of health. Men whom I certainly could not pronounce unreasonable would uphold it as a first installment of a general regulation of the hours of work.[27]

In a book written in 2011, former Supreme Court Justice John Paul Stevens said, *Lochner* "is the case in which Justice Oliver Wendell Holmes wrote the most influential dissenting opinion in the Court's history."[28]

In future statements, Holmes would continue to express the theme of judicial restraint. In a 1913 speech he said:

It is a misfortune if a judge reads his conscious or unconscious sympathy with one side or the other prematurely into the law, and forgets that what seem to him to be first principles are believed by half his fellow men to be wrong... Judges are apt to be naïf [sic], simple-minded men... We too need education in the obvious — to learn to *transcend our own convictions* and to leave room for much that we hold dear to be done away with short of revolution by the orderly change of law.[29]

---

[27] *Ibid.*, emphasis added.

[28] John Paul Stevens, *Five Chiefs: A Supreme Court Memoir* (New York, 2011), 25.

[29] Oliver Wendell Holmes, "Law and the Court," speech to Harvard Law School Association of New York, February 15, 1913, pp. 98, 101–102, cited

In 1921, Benjamin N. Cardozo — who would later replace Holmes on the Supreme Court — discussed what *Lochner* meant. He began by referring to a judge who had asserted that the 1883 argument of *Hurtado v. California*[30] was "the dawn of a new epoch." Continuing, Cardozo wrote:

> If the new epoch had then dawned, it was still obscured by fog and cloud. Scattered rays of light may have heralded the coming day. They were not enough to blaze a path. Even as late as 1905, the decision in *Lochner v. New York* ... still spoke in terms untouched by the light of the new spirit. It is the dissenting opinion of Justice Holmes, which men will turn to in the future as the beginning of an era.[31]

The durability of Holmes's doctrine of judicial restraint may be seen in the recent decision in *National Federation of Independent Businesses v. Sebelius*,[32] in which the Supreme Court upheld the constitutionality of Congress's Patient Protection and Affordable Care Act adopted to provide health-insurance coverage. Chief Justice John Roberts "quoted one of his heroes, Justice Oliver Wendell Holmes, Jr.," in embracing judicial restraint as explained by Holmes in his *Lochner v. New York* dissent.[33]

---

in Felix Frankfurter, "Constitutional Opinions of Justice Holmes," *Harvard Law Review 29* (1915–1916): 683, 691.

[30] 110 U.S. 516 (1883).

[31] Benjamin N. Cardozo, *The Nature of the Judicial Process* (New Haven, 1921), 79.

[32] 132 S. Ct. 2566 (2012).

[33] *See* Jeffrey Rosen, "John Roberts, the Umpire in Chief," *The New York Times*, June 28, 2015, p. 4; *see also* David G. Savage, "Chief Justice is Full of Surprises," *Los Angeles Times*, Sept. 29, 2015, pp. A–1, 8 (citing Chief

One scholar, in a well-written article on Holmes, has oddly misconstrued one of Holmes's central virtues: his extraordinary ability to detach his personal views from his judicial opinions. The article refers to Holmes's dissent in *Vegelahn v. Guntner*, while serving on the Massachusetts Supreme Judicial Court, and states that the dissent "furthered his unwarranted reputation as a friend of labor." Then the author refers to Holmes's "most famous dissent" in *Lochner*, and says Holmes's dissent was "again not out of sympathy for workers."[34] The point the author missed is that Holmes *never* substituted his personal views on the *wisdom* of legislation for those of legislators, whether he sympathized with labor, capital, or any other interest. The article illustrates how the most scholarly of writers may fail to understand how scrupulous Holmes was in divorcing his personal views from his judicial work.

Vindication of Holmes's thought in *Lochner* would not come in his lifetime. The Supreme Court continued to invalidate statutes, state and federal, based on the majority's idea of "economic liberty." From 1899 to 1937, decisions under the 14th Amendment due process and equal protection clauses held 159 state statutes unconstitutional.[35]

Justice Roberts's "commitment to judicial restraint"); see also [as of December 20, 2016] *King v. Burwell*, 135 S. Ct. 2480, 192 L. Ed. 2nd 483, 83 U.S.L.W. 4541 (2015) (majority opinion of the Chief Justice, again upholding the constitutionality of the Affordable Care Act).

[34] Henry Cohen, "Oliver Wendell Holmes, Jr.: Life and Philosophy," *The Federal Lawyer* (New York, *The New York Times*, January 2004), 23–25. When he wrote the article, Cohen was a legislative attorney with the Congressional Research Service of the Library of Congress.

[35] Edward L. Barrett, *et alia*, *Constitutional Law* (Brooklyn, 1963), 932.

In the 1930's, the Court's ideological decisions under the 14th Amendment repeatedly declared unconstitutional President Franklin D. Roosevelt's New Deal legislation. FDR eventually made serious and credible threats to "pack the Court" with new justices if the Court did not relent. Finally, in 1937, came "the switch in time that saved nine:" Justice Owen Roberts switched his vote in the 1937 case *West Coast Hotel Co. v. Parrish*.[36] Chief Justice Charles Evan Hughes assigned the opinion to himself and disavowed the old "liberty of contract dogma."[37] Other 1937 decisions followed, abandoning the *laissez faire* doctrine and "freedom of contract" rationale for protecting business interests at the expense of all other interests. It took 31 years, but two years after his death, Holmes had been vindicated.

---

[36] 300 U.S. 379 (1937).
[37] Burns, *Packing the Court*, 149.

Rosika Schwimmer, c. 1910.
(*Courtesy of Library of Congress*)

11

SPEECH

"Freedom for the thought that we hate."

PROFESSORS AND SCHOLARS have minutely scrutinized Holmes's early 20th-century First Amendment decisions. They have sifted his words, often seeking a new slant, or even hoping to find error. For these legal archeologists, error is the equivalent of a holy grail.

In their quest for something new or startling, some of these writers have themselves fallen into error. The perspective of the professor has not always been adequate to see what would be obvious to a veteran of the courtroom. Holmes's 1919 opinions will illustrate the point.

The year 1919 saw four Espionage Act cases decided by the Supreme Court that would permanently change the meaning of the First Amendment. The Espionage Act was adopted by Congress in 1917 to prevent interference with the draft in the pending World War. In the first three cases Holmes wrote opinions for a unanimous court. In all three of those cases the Court upheld charges of violating or attempting to violate the Espionage Act by conduct and speech that interfered with recruiting for the Army.

In the first case, *Schenck v. United States*,[1] Socialist Party officials circulated a leaflet to men who had been drafted to

---

[1] 249 U.S. 47 (1919).

serve in the Army. The document declared that "conscription was despotism in its worst form and a monstrous wrong against humanity in the interest of Wall Street's chosen few." It urged drafted soldiers, "Do not submit to intimidation," and "assert your rights." The men were indicted on charges based solely on speech, alleging a conspiracy to violate the Espionage Act by "causing and attempting to cause" obstruction of the war effort. There was no evidence, or even allegation, that defendants had succeeded in obstructing the war effort. But, the government argued, defendants intended, conspired, and attempted to interfere. Their circular asked draftees not to submit to the draft, and, the government claimed, the language of the circular had a "tendency" to obstruct the war effort.

In a typically short, three-page opinion for a unanimous court, Holmes saw the case as a simple attempt and conspiracy to violate the Espionage Act. He reasoned that, "Of course the document would not have been sent unless it had been intended to have some effect, and we do not see what effect it could be expected to have upon persons subject to the draft except to influence them to obstruct the carrying of it out. The defendants do not deny that the jury might find against them on this point."[2]

Next, Holmes asked whether, despite defendants' conspiracy and attempt to obstruct the war effort, their conduct in passing out the leaflets was protected by the First Amendment. The answer, said Holmes, depended entirely upon the circumstances surrounding the defendants' conduct.

---

[2] *Ibid.*, 51.

He said, "We admit that in many places and in ordinary times the defendants in saying all that was said in the circular would have been within their constitutional rights."[3] Holmes then wrote one of the most recognizable and influential paragraphs in the history of constitutional law:

> But the character of every act depends upon the circumstances in which it is done.... The most stringent protection of free speech would not protect a man in *falsely shouting fire in a theater and causing a panic* .... The question in every case is whether the words are used in such circumstances and are of such a nature as to create a *clear and present danger* that they will bring about the substantive evils that Congress has a right to prevent. It is a question of proximity and degree ... If the act (speaking, or circulating a paper), its tendency and the intent with which it is done are the same, we perceive no ground for saying that success alone warrants making the act a crime.[4]

As Holmes explained, the law of criminal attempt was well settled. Congress may properly punish, say, a conspiracy or attempt to commit murder as well as murder itself. It is hardly necessary to wait until the planned crime is actually committed. Moreover, the fact that a defendant uses words in attempting to commit the substantive crime does not immunize him from punishment. In *Schenck,* the defendants' use of words in trying to obstruct the draft, instead of employing some other means, did not make their conduct any

---

[3] *Ibid.,* 52.
[4] *Ibid.*

less an attempt to obstruct. Crimes may be committed with speech as well as with acts. Indeed, the crime of conspiracy, virtually by definition, is committed by using speech. Aiding and abetting a perpetrator with words of encouragement, and in that way attempting to commit a crime, are other examples of crimes often committed by words.

Holmes's point was simple: the mere use of words in committing crimes does not grant the perpetrator immunity from prosecution.

Holmes disliked absolutes in legal principles. Acts and words should be viewed in the context in which they arise. Their meaning changes as the circumstances change. As Holmes often explained, "It is a question of proximity and degree." Turn a kaleidoscope slightly and a different view is seen. In peacetime, words used by a defendant may be harmless. In war, the significance of the same words may change.

Holmes's language in *Schenck* provided a kind of tool kit containing a test for deciding whether conduct or speech is a punishable crime: the issue is whether the speech or conduct creates a "clear and present danger" of bringing about the "substantive evils that Congress has a right to prevent." That kind of speech does not deserve First Amendment protection. Falsely shouting fire in a crowded theater causing a panic is not protected speech. But falsely shout fire in an empty theater and the picture changes.

Holmes's reasoning in *Schenck* was typical of his finely nuanced thought. The meanings of words are not fixed. They may change dramatically depending on the circumstances in which they are used. In another context, Holmes expressed this thought: "A word is not a crystal, transparent and unchanged; it is the skin of a living thought and may vary greatly in color and content according to the circumstances and the times in which it is used."[5]

Frohwerk v. U.S.,[6] the next 1919 Espionage Act case, involved defendants who published newspaper articles criticizing the war effort, calling it "outright murder." The articles issued "words of warning to the American people," while offering compliments to Germany, and declaring, "We say therefore, cease firing."[7]

As he had in *Schenck*, Holmes found that the defendants had properly been convicted of a criminal attempt to obstruct the war effort. Again he held that under the circumstances involved, conviction for speech did not violate the First Amendment. He acknowledged that, "We do not lose our right to condemn either measures or men because the Country is at war."[8] But on the record presented, "it is impossible to say that it might not have been found that the circulation of the [defendants'] paper was in quarters where a little breath would be enough to kindle a flame and that the fact was known and relied upon by those who sent the paper out."[9] Thus, the Court unanimously affirmed defendants' convictions.

The third 1919 Espionage Act case, *Debs v. U.S.*,[10] would become the most controversial of the first three. Eugene Debs, the Socialist Party candidate for president in 1912, was charged

---

[5] *Towne v. Eisner* 245 U.S. 418, 425 (1918).
[6] 249 U.S. 204 (1919).
[7] *Ibid.*, 207.
[8] *Ibid.*, 208.
[9] *Ibid.*, 209.
[10] 249 U. S. 211 (1919).

with making a speech advocating socialism which caused, incited, and attempted to cause disloyalty to the United States and obstruction of the recruiting and enlistment service. Although focusing on socialism, Debs's speech referred to three "loyal comrades" who were then serving time in a workhouse for aiding and abetting a person in failing to register for the draft. Holmes pointed out that Debs "said he had to be prudent and might not have been able to say all that he thought, thus intimating to his hearers that they might infer that he meant more."[11] Debs, said Holmes, "praised [another socialist] for her loyalty to Socialism ... and said that she was convicted [of espionage] on false testimony ... ."[12]

At his trial, Debs "presented no witnesses, only the defendant himself, who spoke for two hours."[13] Debs referred to an "Anti-War Proclamation and Program" which said that "capitalism was the cause of the war," the declaration of war by the United States was "a crime against the people of the United States," and recommended continuous opposition to the war by "demonstrations, mass petitions and all other means within our power."[14]

The court convicted Debs of violations of the Espionage Act and the trial court sentenced him to ten years in prison.

Holmes's opinion, again for a unanimous court, affirmed the convictions. Holmes wrote that, as in *Schenck* and *Frohwerk*, the question was whether the "natural and

---

[11] *Ibid.*, 213.
[12] *Ibid.*
[13] A. Scott Berg, *Wilson* (New York, 2013), 496.
[14] *Debs v. U. S. supra*, 215–216.

Eugene Debs leaves the White House on December 26, 1921, after having a 30 minute conversation with President Warren G. Harding who had commuted his ten year sentence. (*Courtesy of Library of Congress*)

intended effect would be to obstruct recruiting."[15] The opinion rejected Debs's contention that the Espionage Act violated the First Amendment. In doing so, Holmes made no mention of the clear and present danger test.

Holmes personally wished it had not been necessary to affirm the convictions. He wrote to Laski, saying "between ourselves I greatly regretted having to write" the opinion. Again saying "between ourselves," Holmes told Laski he hoped President Wilson would issue a pardon.[16]

---

[15] *Ibid.*, 215.
[16] Howe (ed.), *Holmes-Laski Letters*, I, 190, March 16, 1919.

Wilson considered Debs a traitor and refused to pardon him. "It galled Wilson that while 'the flower of American youth was pouring out its blood to vindicate the cause of civilization, this man, Debs, stood behind the lines, sniping, attacking and denouncing them.'"[17] In 1921, President Warren G. Harding commuted Debs's sentence to "time served" and released him.

Following the *Debs* decision, a firestorm of criticism erupted. An article by the noted American legal scholar Ernst Freund in the May 3, 1919 issue of *The New Republic* lamented that "the jury was permitted to find a tendency and an intent to obstruct recruiting."[18] But why should that be objectionable? Juries decide the issue of intent every day. Finding "tendency," or probability, is also within the competence of a jury. Was Freund actually questioning the right to a jury trial in First Amendment cases? He did not say. Instead, he wrote, "I shall not attempt to determine what in the way of restraint is possible under the First Amendment."[19] But he did not hesitate to criticize the justices who did have to decide such issues. His criticism included the statement that "to be permitted to agitate at your own peril, subject to a jury's guessing at motive, tendency and possible effect, makes the right to free speech a precarious gift."[20] This statement strongly suggests that Freund believed the Constitutional right to a jury trial should not be available to decide facts in

---

[17] Berg, *Wilson*, 496.
[18] Ernst Freund, "The Debs Case and Freedom of Speech," *The New Republic*, May 3, 1919, 13.
[19] *Ibid.*
[20] *Ibid.*, 14.

such a case on the ground a jury would have been "guessing" in making determinations that juries routinely make.

Freund next appeared to reveal his real, underlying, objection. He wrote, "Surely implied provocation in connection with *political offenses* is an unsafe doctrine if it has to be made plausible by a parallel so manifestly inappropriate [as the clear-and-present-danger standard]."[21] Thus, what Freund termed "political offenses," a category in which he would include attempting to obstruct the nation's war effort, should be held immune from judicial review. That view has never enjoyed any legal support, then or since.

An Afterword to Freund's article, published in the 1973 issue of the *University of Chicago Law Review* by Douglas H. Ginsburg,[22] discussed with approval U. S. District Court Judge Learned Hand's decision in *Masses Publishing Co. v. Patten*.[23] Construing the same section of the Espionage Act as the one under which Debs was convicted, Judge Hand held that, "If one stops short of urging upon others that it is their duty or their interest to resist the law, it seems to me one should not be held to have attempted to cause the violation." Otherwise, "every political agitation which can be shown to be apt to create a seditious temper is illegal."[24]

Hand wrote to Holmes after the *Debs* decision urging that his own test be applied: responsibility for words would begin

---

[21] *Ibid.*, emphasis added.
[22] Douglas H. Ginsburg, "Afterword," *University of Chicago Law Review*, Vol. 40, number 2, Winter 1973.
[23] 244 Fed. 535 (1917), reversed in *Masses Publishing Co. v. Patten*, 245 Fed. 102 (C.C.A. 2nd 1917).
[24] 244 Fed. 535 ff., *supra*.

only "when the words were directly an incitement." This was a surprising statement, especially coming from the highly-respected Judge Hand. Without saying so, he appeared to want to categorically revise, if not eliminate, long-settled law governing criminal attempts where "political agitation" was involved. Criminal attempts are committed where an accused takes a step toward committing a crime with the intent to commit the crime.[25] But Hand's test would assign criminal responsibility for words only "when the words were directly an incitement."

Holmes did not agree. In a letter to Hand, he said, regarding "intent under the Espionage Act, I believe I have said nothing except to note that under the instructions the *jury* must be taken to have found that Debs's speech was intended to obstruct and tended to obstruct...." Here Holmes recognized that the issues of intent and tendency to obstruct were questions to be decided solely by the jury. Holmes referred to Hand's *Masses* decision and said, "I take it that you agree that words may constitute an obstruction within the statute, even without proof that the obstruction was successful to the point of preventing recruiting. That I at least think plain."[26]

Indeed, Hand had conceded in *Masses* that "words may constitute an obstruction ... without preventing."[27] Given that concession, what would satisfy Hand's "direct advocacy of resistance" test? Possibly he meant "direct advocacy" required

---

[25] See, *e.g.*, Rollin M. Perkins, *Perkins on Criminal Law* (Brooklyn, 1957), 176–177.
[26] White, *Justice Oliver Wendell Holmes*, 425–426, 577n.
[27] 244 Fed. 535ff., *supra*.

"direct" — in contrast to circumstantial — evidence. But in virtually every other context circumstantial evidence is regarded as sufficient to prove criminal offenses, including the most serious and heinous of crimes, such as first-degree murder among countless others. "Direct" evidence would include a confession that the defendant intended by his speech to interfere with recruiting. But a confession is hardly the only reliable evidence of intent. Evidence of pretrial confessions is often the least reliable evidence.

Of course the speaker could explicitly tell his audience that "I am here to convince you to evade the draft." Aside from the improbability of such a public confession, a rule limiting evidence of obstruction or attempted obstruction to private or public admissions would ignore the many, more-subtle, words of encouragement that might be used by the skilled speaker, someone like Debs. Hand did not address that possibility. The meaning of his "direct-advocacy" test remains unclear.

Employing subtle words of persuasion was addressed by Freund in his 1919 article in *The New Republic*. He said, "An experienced speaker like Debs knows the effect of words. He must have known that, while he might keep alive and even create disaffection, his power to create actual obstruction to a compulsory draft was practically nil, and he could hardly have intended what he could not hope to achieve; in fact it is difficult to conceive of a form of obstruction that can be opposed to a compulsory draft."[28] This was an interesting statement by someone who claimed that a jury would be

---

[28] Ernst Freund, "The Debs Case and Freedom of Speech," *The New Republic*, Vol. 19 Issue 235 (May 1919), 14.

"*guessing* at motive, tendency and possible effect...," while simultaneously asserting what Debs "*must have known.*"

Freund was doing exactly what a judge may not do in reviewing a decision of a jury: he was substituting his personal view of what Debs "intended" for that of the jury. Of course a writer is free to do that. But criticism of an appellate judge for doing so reveals a lack of understanding of the role of the judge.

Further, why would a speech by Debs, the "experienced speaker," have a "practically nil" power to create actual obstruction? And could his speech have been an *attempt* to create actual obstruction? Freund did not discuss these obvious questions though Debs had been convicted of both obstruction and an attempt to obstruct.

In his 1973 Afterword to the Freund article, Ginsburg made clear that, "Freund, of course, would not have admitted of even a narrow exception for a doctrine of 'indirect provocation, i.e., implied or inferential incitement.'"[29] As Holmes wrote to Herbert Croly, the editor of *The New Republic*, on May 12, 1919, "Freund's objection to a jury 'guessing at motive, tendency and possible effect' is an objection to pretty much the whole body of the law, which for thirty years I have made my brethren smile by insisting to be everywhere a matter of degree."[30]

The criticism of Holmes's *Debs* opinion included a June 1919 article by Zechariah Chafee, "Freedom of Speech in

---

[29] Ginsburg, "Afterword," *supra*.
[30] Quoted in Howe (ed.), *Holmes-Laski Letters*, I, 203.

Wartime."³¹ Chafee, then an assistant professor of law at Harvard Law School, described the purpose of his lengthy article in sweeping terms: "[T]o ascertain the nature and scope of the policy which finds expression in the First Amendment to the United States Constitution and the similar clauses of all the state constitutions, and then to determine the place of that policy in the conduct of war, and particularly the war with Germany."³²

Chafee explained his conception of free speech: "The true meaning of freedom of speech seems to be this. One of the most important purposes of society and government is the discovery and spread of truth on subjects of general concern. This is possible only through absolutely unlimited discussion...."³³

Chafee did recognize that unlimited discussion "sometimes interferes with [other constitutional] purposes, which must then be balanced against freedom of speech, but freedom of speech ought to weigh heavily in the scale."³⁴ Continuing, Chafee said that Holmes, "[t]he judge who has done most to bring social interests into legal thinking said years ago, 'I think that judges themselves have failed adequately to recognize their duty of weighing considerations of social advantage [which] is simply to leave the very ground and foundations of judgment inarticulate and often unconscious.'"³⁵

---

[31] Zechariah Chafee, "Freedom of Speech in Wartime," *Harvard Law Review* 32 (1919), 932.
[32] *Ibid.*, 935.
[33] *Ibid.*, 956.
[34] *Ibid.*, 957.
[35] *Ibid.*, 959, citing Holmes, "The Path of the Law," 457, 467.

Chafee concluded in his article that, "If the Supreme Court had applied [the] same standard of 'clear and present danger' to the utterances of Eugene V. Debs, ... it is hard to see how he could have been held guilty."[36] As we shall see, in 1941 Chafee answered his own concern. Over time, he would not only understand the reason for Holmes's *Debs* opinion. He would fully embrace it himself.

In the final Espionage Act case decided in 1919, a dissent by Holmes would eventually become the very definition of the First Amendment.

Jacob Abrams (right) and Russian émigrés, charged with espionage, who were at the center of the Court's 1919 decision in *Abrams v. United States*.
(*Unidentified newspaper photo*)

---

[36] Chafee, "Freedom of Speech in Wartime," 967–968.

The majority opinion in *Abrams v. U.S.*,[37] written by Justice John H. Clark, affirmed convictions of five defendants for conspiring and attempting to violate the Act, as amended in 1918. The 1918 amendment created new offenses which included "uttering, printing, writing, or publishing any disloyal, profane, scurrilous, or abusive language intended to incite resistance to the United States or to promote the cause of its enemies; or any language urging curtailment of production of any things necessary to the prosecution of the war with the intent to hinder such prosecution."[38]

Defendants, who had been born in Russia, were charged with distributing in New York some 5,000 copies of leaflets printed in English and Yiddish intended to encourage resistance to the then-pending war with Germany. Three of the defendants testified they were "rebels," "revolutionists," "anarchists," [and] "that they did not believe in government in any form."[39] One leaflet denounced President Wilson as "a hypocrite and a coward because troops were sent into Russia." A circular asserted, "The Russian Revolution cries: Workers of the World! Awake! Rise! Put down your enemy and mine!"[40] The *Abrams* majority decision construed the circulars as an appeal to workers "to arise and put down by force the government of the United States."[41]

Holmes dissented. In joining the dissent, Justice Brandeis wrote to Holmes, "I join you heartily and gratefully. This is fine

---

[37] 250 U.S. 616 (1919).
[38] *Ibid.*, 617–618.
[39] *Ibid.*, 620.
[40] *Ibid.*
[41] *Ibid.*, 618.

— very."[42] Holmes's dissent virtually created modern First Amendment doctrine. "Clear and present danger" now became the keystone for testing whether speech could be punished.

After summarizing the contents of the leaflets, Holmes noted that in one circular defendants "do urge curtailment of production of things necessary to the prosecution of the war within the meaning of the [Espionage] Act as amended in 1918." But to make the conduct criminal, Holmes said, the statute requires that the conduct should be done "'with intent by such curtailment to cripple or hinder the U. S. in the prosecution of the war.' It seems to me that no such intent is proved."[43]

Explaining the absence of proof, Holmes reasoned that the statute "must be taken to use its words in a strict and accurate sense. They would be absurd in any other."[44] He offered an example of why the words must be strictly construed to avoid an absurd result: "A patriot might think that we were wasting money on aeroplanes, or making more cannon of a certain kind than we needed, and might advocate curtailment with success, yet even if it turned out that the curtailment hindered and was thought by other minds to have been obviously likely to hinder the United States in the prosecution of the war, no one would hold such conduct a crime."[45] This conclusion seems unassailable.

Holmes then paused to revisit the first three 1919 decisions to make clear that "I never have seen any reason to doubt that the *questions of law that alone were before this*

---

[42] Urofsky, *Louis D. Brandeis*, 553.
[43] *Abrams v. U.S., supra*, 626.
[44] *Ibid.*, 627.
[45] *Ibid.*

Court in the cases of *Schenck...*, *Frohwerk...*, and *Debs...*, were rightly decided."[46] Those three cases, he pointed out, involved *only questions of law.*

This was a critical point. Legally, there is a wide divide between questions of law and questions of fact. *Questions of law* are decided solely by the judge. *Questions of fact* are decided solely by the "trier of fact," either a jury in a jury trial or the trial judge in a non-jury case. But since appellate judges do not see and hear witnesses, they are unable to evaluate the witnesses' credibility. Therefore, they must not engage in "fact finding," substituting their views of the facts for the facts found by the jury or trial judge.

Stated differently, the appellate court may not decide the "what-happened." For instance, did a driver run a red light? Did a person fire a gun? Did a person have the requisite intent or other state of mind to commit a certain crime? The appellate court is limited to determining the *legal consequences* of running a red light, or firing a gun, or acting with intent, as found by the jury or trial judge. These were the kinds of factual issues *decided by the juries* in the first three 1919 cases. The Supreme Court was bound to honor these factual determinations.

Holmes thought that "Congress certainly cannot forbid *all effort* to change the mind of the country. Now nobody can suppose that the surreptitious publishing of a silly leaflet by an unknown man, without more, would present any immediate danger that its opinions would hinder the success of the government arms or have any appreciable tendency to

---

[46] *Ibid.*, emphasis added.

do so."[47] Indeed, what would be left of the First Amendment in wartime if *no criticism* of the war effort is allowed?

Looking at the statutory elements of the charged crimes, Holmes pointed out that to constitute an attempt to commit the substantive offense of espionage, an "actual intent" to hinder the war effort against Germany was required. But the *Abrams* defendants intended only "to *help Russia* and stop American intervention there against the popular government — not to impede the United States in the war that it was carrying on" against *Germany*.[48] Defendants asserted that, "It is absurd to call us pro-German. We hate and despise German militarism more than do you tyrants. We have more reason to denounce German militarism than has the coward of the White House."[49]

Defendants' pro-Russia objective, Holmes said, "seems to me by no means enough to show an attempt to produce that effect" of impeding the war effort against Germany.[50]

Holmes distinguished the *Abrams* circumstances from those in the three earlier 1919 cases. Abrams was an "unknown man" who published a "silly leaflet." In contrast, the *Schenck* Socialist-Party defendants targeted draftees with their leaflets, encouraging them to refuse to submit to the "despotic" draft. In *Frohwerk*, the defendants published a newspaper condemning the war effort. And in *Debs*, the speech was made by the well-known candidate for president

---

[47] *Ibid.*, 628, emphasis added.
[48] *Ibid.*, 629, emphasis added.
[49] *Ibid.*, 625.
[50] *Ibid.*, 629.

on the Socialist Party ticket. In all three cases the conduct reached wide audiences and could have succeeded in interfering with recruiting or the draft.

Further, Holmes charged that "the defendants are to be made to suffer not for what the indictment alleges but for the *creed* that they avow, [one that] *no one has a right even to consider* in dealing with the charges before the court."[51] Here Holmes declared that no one may constitutionally be prosecuted for believing in or advocating a particular creed, a critical facet of the First Amendment.

Holmes now gathered himself to write for the ages. His soaring eloquence still defines the meaning of the First Amendment nearly 100 years later.

> *Persecution for the expression of opinions* seems to me to be perfectly logical. If you have no doubt of your premises or your power and want a certain result with all your heart you naturally express your wishes in law and sweep away all opposition. To allow opposition by speech seems to indicate that you think the speech impotent, as when a man says that he has squared the circle...or that you doubt either your power or your premises. But when men have realized that *time has upset many fighting faiths*, they may come to believe even more than they believe the very foundations of their own conduct that the ultimate good desired is better reached by *free trade in ideas — the best test of truth is the power of the thought to get itself accepted*

---

[51] *Ibid.*, 629–630, emphasis added.

in the competition of the market, and that *truth* is the only ground upon which their wishes can safely be carried out.[52]

Holmes's phrase — "the competition of the market" — has endlessly fascinated scholars. The *Abrams* dissent has been described as "the canonical opinion that gave rise to the arresting figure of the "marketplace of ideas" ... The *Abrams* dissent's "peroration articulates in a single paragraph a highly sophisticated if cryptic philosophical justification for the freedom of speech."[53]

Holmes finished his *Abrams* dissent by defining the Constitution itself:

> That at any rate is the theory of our Constitution. It is an experiment, as all life is an experiment. Every year if not every day we have to wager our salvation upon some prophecy based upon imperfect knowledge. While that experiment is part of our system I think that we should be eternally vigilant against attempts to check the expression of *opinions that we loathe* and believe to be fraught with death, unless they *so imminently threaten immediate interference* with the lawful and pressing purposes of the law that an immediate check is necessary to save the country.[54]

In the light of these words, his final phrase was startling, like Lincoln's phrasing at Gettysburg — "The world will little

---

[52] *Ibid.*, 630, emphasis added.
[53] Vincent Blasi, "Holmes and the Marketplace of Ideas," *The Supreme Court Review* 1(2004), 2–3.
[54] *Abrams v. U.S., supra* 630, emphasis added.

note, nor long remember what we say here...." Holmes's final phrase was no less stirring for its modesty: "... I regret that I cannot put into more impressive words my belief that in their conviction upon this indictment the defendants were deprived of rights under the Constitution of the United States."[55]

Many of Holmes's former critics now gushed with praise. Chafee was ecstatic. In his later book, *Free Speech in the United States*, first published in 1941, he recalled how "grieved" he and others had been by Holmes's *Debs* opinion. "Looking backward, however, we see that Justice Holmes was biding his time until the Court should have before it a conviction so clearly wrong as to let him speak out his deepest thoughts about the First Amendment."[56] That case was *Abrams*. Speaking of Holmes's clear-and-present danger test, Chafee said that "this principle is greatly strengthened since the *Abrams* case by Justice Holmes's magnificent exposition of the philosophic basis of this article of our Constitution ...."[57]

Chafee's admiration for Holmes affords an excellent example of how even the most recent scholars confuse Holmes's influence on other prominent thinkers with what they claim is the exact opposite. Lynne Olson's 2013 book *Those Angry Days: Roosevelt, Lindbergh, and America's Fight over World War II, 1939–1941* — which in turn relies on a 1999 study of free speech during wartime by Richard W. Steele — is a case in point: "Heavily influenced by Chafee's

---

[55] *Ibid.*, 631.
[56] Zechariah Chafee, Jr., *Free Speech in the United States* (Cambridge, Massachusetts, 1941), 86.
[57] *Ibid.*, 136.

writings," asserts Olson, "Holmes argued that 'a clear and present danger' to law and security must exist before speech can legally be curbed by the state." Chafee's 1941 gush for Holmes's *Abrams* dissent suggests that Chafee was "heavily influenced" by Holmes, and not the reverse.[58]

Other Holmes admirers added their praise of Holmes's *Abrams* dissent. Harold Laski, who had scarcely been able to conceal his disappointment in Holmes's opinion in *Debs,* wrote that no opinion of Holmes was "superior either in nobility or outlook, in dignity of phrasing .... It is a fine and moving document for which I am deeply and happily grateful."[59]

Holmes's friend Felix Frankfurter, then a Harvard Law School professor, later a Supreme Court justice, told Holmes with "gratitude and, may I say it, the pride I have in your dissent," in which "you lift the voice of the noble human spirit."[60]

Numerous others contacted Holmes to express admiration for his dissent.

Some chroniclers of Holmes have asserted that Holmes's *Abrams* dissent represented a change of mind after he had written the first three 1919 opinions.[61]

---

[58] Lynne Olson, *Those Angry Days: Roosevelt, Lindbergh, and America's Fight over World War II, 1939–1941* (New York, 2013), 107; Olson in turn cited Richard W. Steele, *Free Speech in the Good War* (New York, 1999), 10.
[59] Howe (ed.), *Holmes-Laski Letters,* I, 220, November 12, 1919.
[60] Mennel and Compston (eds.), *Holmes and Frankfurter: Their Correspondence 1912–1934,* p. 75, November 12, 1919.
[61] *See, e.g.,* White, *Justice Oliver Wendell Holmes,* 432–433, 436 (insisting that the *Abrams* dissent was an "abandonment" of Holmes's previous view of criminal attempt, and was a "reformulation" of both his conception of

As seen, Holmes explained in *Abrams* that he had "never seen any reason to doubt that *questions of law alone* were before this Court" in *Schenck, Frohwerk,* and *Debs,* and that they "were rightly decided."[62] To speculate that Holmes had changed his views in *Abrams* is to suggest that he did not believe what he said in his dissent, that only questions of law were involved in *Schenck, Frohwerk,* and *Debs,* and that those cases were rightly decided. Or the change-of-mind advocates may not have recognized the significance of Holmes's explanation that *only questions of law* were presented in those three cases. They also appear to ignore Holmes's opinion that the facts in *Debs* "*warrant the jury in finding* that one purpose of Debs's speech ... was to oppose not only war in general but this war, and that the opposition was so expressed that its *natural and intended effect* would be to obstruct recruiting."[63] As discussed, since the facts Holmes mentioned were jury questions, the Supreme Court was bound by the jury's decisions.

A precursor of Holmes's 1919 opinions in the speech cases plainly refutes the claim that he changed his mind in *Abrams.*[64] "Historical evidence," writes scholar Sheldon Novick, "shows

---

the First Amendment and of the clear and present danger test); Thomas Healy, *The Great Dissent: How Oliver Wendell Holmes Changed His Mind — and Changed the History of Free Speech in America* (New York, 2013), 198 *et seq.* (speculating that possibly, "thanks to the arguments of Hand and Freund, Holmes was simply no longer willing to grant juries the same latitude as before"); Urofsky, *Louis D. Brandeis,* 553 ("no single factor led to the about face" by Holmes and Brandeis).

[62] *Abrams v. U.S., supra,* 627, emphasis added.
[63] *Debs v. U.S., supra,* 214–215, emphasis added.
[64] *See* Sheldon Novick, "The Unrevised Holmes and Freedom of Expression," *The Supreme Court Review* (1991), 304–305, 317.

without much doubt that Holmes's views did not change, and that *Schenck* and *Abrams* were cut from the same bolt."[65] In *Baltzer v. United States*,[66] three men were convicted of acting and conspiring to obstruct the draft and enlistment service. They sent a petition to the Governor of South Dakota demanding that he prevent incurring any expenses to support the draft by the United States unless the expenses could be paid for in cash, and making other, similar demands designed to affect recruiting and the draft. They threatened that if the Governor refused to exercise these supposed powers he would be defeated at the polls. Of course the Governor had no power to take any of the actions demanded. All such powers were vested in the federal government.

The case arrived in the Supreme Court during its October 1918 term. Seven justices were prepared to affirm the convictions. Holmes wrote a typically short, unpublished dissent in which Brandeis joined. Holmes began by questioning how the petition could possibly influence the draft:

> It seems to me that this [is a] petition to an official by ignorant persons who suppose him to possess power of revision and change that he does not ...[and] was nothing but the foolish exercise of a right [presumably to petition the government under the First Amendment] .... I cannot see how asking a change in the mode of administering the draft so as to make it accord with what is supposed to be required by law can be said to obstruct it. I cannot see how combining

---

[65] *Ibid.*, 304.
[66] 248 U.S. 593 (1918); *cf.* White, *Justice Oliver Wendell Holmes*, 414, 573n.

to do it is conspiracy to do anything that citizens have not a perfect right to do. It is apparent on the face of the paper that it assumes the power to be in the person addressed. I should have supposed that an article in a newspaper advocating these same things would have left untouched the sensibilities even of those most afraid of free speech.

Continuing, Holmes celebrated our constitutional freedoms:

We have enjoyed so much freedom for so long that perhaps we are in danger of forgetting that the bill of rights which cost so much blood to establish still is worth fighting for, and that no title of it should be abridged unconstitutionally in those cases of subsequent punishment with which this court has had to deal from time to time. But the emergency would have to be very great before I could be persuaded that an appeal for political action through legal channels, addressed to those supposed to have power to take such action, was an act that the Constitution did not protect as well after as before.

Handwritten notes by Chief Justice Edward Douglass White, Jr., made at the time, reflect that Holmes's dissent caused the Chief Justice concern. He apparently wanted a unanimous decision in this first espionage case.[67]

The only published opinion in *Baltzer* is a remarkable one-sentence statement by the Court: "Judgment reversed,

---

[67] White, *Justice Oliver Wendell Holmes*, 573 (notes 11, 12, 13), citing Sheldon Novick, "Justice Holmes and the Art of Biography," *William & Mary Law Review* 33 (1992): 1219, 1230.

upon *confession of error*; and cause remanded for further proceedings in accordance with law."[68] There is no evidence why the Solicitor General of the United States, who represented the Government, confessed error. The likely reason is that he thought the Government's case was weak and therefore *Baltzer* was the wrong case to rely upon to test the constitutionality of the Espionage Act. The other espionage cases were scheduled for argument in January 1919 and may have been thought much stronger for the Government's position than *Baltzer*. In the event, as we have seen, the Government succeeded: the Supreme Court affirmed convictions in all four of the 1919 cases.

Of further significance is that Holmes's unpublished dissent demonstrated beyond doubt that he arrived at his First Amendment views quite on his own. He had no need to be enlightened by the articles of Chafee and Freund attacking his *Debs* decision, both written after his dissent in *Baltzer*.

Returning to Holmes's *Abrams* dissent, as seen it drew high praise from many sources, but there were detractors. One in particular was surprising. John H. Wigmore was a celebrated scholar and professor, later dean, at Northwestern University Law School. He published dozens of books on various legal subjects and his book on the law of evidence is viewed as a classic.

In 1920, Wigmore published a lengthy article in the *Illinois Law Review* denouncing Holmes's *Abrams* dissent. The fervor of his condemnation is suggested in the title:

---

[68] *Baltzer v. U.S., supra*, 593, emphasis added.

"Abrams v. U.S: Freedom of Speech and Freedom of Thuggery in War-Time and Peace-Time."[69]

The article begins in irrelevance. Wigmore expresses his detestation of "the Workers' Soviets, captained by Lenine [sic] and Trotsky — [which] represents the introduction of a dictatorship of force and violence. It is not a movement of genuine liberty-lovers, but a regime of destruction of property, overthrow of religion, and enthronement of class hatred."[70] But these are uncontested sentiments. Holmes's dissent hardly championed the Bolshevik cause. Holmes has been termed a "Hoover Republican." He certainly did not embrace the cause of Bolshevism. And whether a judge personally agrees or disagrees with speech has nothing to do with his duty as a judge to decide legal issues. Indeed, Holmes has been rightly celebrated for his unfailing refusal to allow his personal views to influence his judicial decisions.

Throughout his article, Wigmore refers to the two dissenters as "the minority of two," or the "Minority Opinion," never naming Holmes and Brandeis. His often-intemperate language stands out: "A pre-existing attitude of the minority disinclined them to interpret the facts as the majority did," we are told.[71] The reference to "the facts" is followed by language denouncing Germany and "the countless unscrupulous inhumanities which marked every step of Germany's

---

[69] John H. Wigmore, "Abrams v. U.S.: Freedom of Speech and Freedom of Thuggery in War-Time and Peace-Time," *Illinois Law Review* XIV (March, 1920), 539.
[70] *Ibid.*, 539–540.
[71] *Ibid.*, 545.

warfare."[72] This statement is made with no recognition that in their circulars Abrams and the other defendants agreed with and fully supported the war against Germany.

The irrelevant discussion continues with lengthy descriptions of the depredations by Germany against various nations. In August 1918, "Abrams and his band of alien parasites" were "cowardly and dastardly" men whose statements "meant a treacherous hamstringing of our citizens-soldiers in the field of France."[73]

The article ridicules the dissent's reasoning that "the ultimate good desired is better reached by free trade in ideas — that the best test of truth is the power of the thought to get itself accepted in the competition of the market." Of this language, Wigmore says, "If these five men could, without the law's restraint, urge munition [*sic*] workers to a general strike and armed violence, then others could lawfully do so; and a thousand disaffected undesirables, aliens and natives alike, were ready and waiting to do so."[74]

Moving, at last, to "The Invocation of Free Speech," Wigmore charged that the Minority Opinion's "attitude of mind, operating subconsciously, must, in consciously and openly justifying itself, invoke some distinct legal principle of universally acknowledged soundness. That is the natural process, deep in human nature, for all of us. What was this saving principle? The constitutional right of Freedom of Speech."[75] The Minority Opinion's "apotheosis of Truth,

---

[72] *Ibid.*, 546.
[73] *Ibid.*, 549.
[74] *Ibid.*, 550.
[75] *Ibid.*

however, shows a blindness to the deadly fact that meantime the 'power of the thought' of these circulars might 'get itself accepted in the competition of the market,' by munitions workers, so as to lose the war …This Opinion, if it had been made the law as a majority opinion, would have ended by our letting soldiers die helpless in France…."[76]

Next the article announces its own rule of law: "Where a nation has definitely committed itself to a foreign war, *all principles of normal internal order may be suspended.* As property may be taken and corporal service may be conscripted, so *liberty of speech may be limited or suppressed,* so far as *deemed needful* for the successful conduct of the war … and *all rights of the individual, and all internal civic interests, become subordinated* to the national right in the struggle for national life."[77]

The article then issues a warning. "The reason, then, that we should view the Minority Opinion with apprehension is that it is symptomatic. Hundreds of well-meaning citizens — 'parlor bolsheviks' and 'pink radicals,' as the phrase goes — are showing a similar complaisance of good-natured tolerance to this licensing of the violence-propaganda."[78]

The article nears its conclusion with language that appears to mock Holmes's opinion, and does so in capital letters:

---

[76] *Ibid.*, 550–551.
[77] *Ibid.*, 552–553, emphasis added.
[78] *Ibid.*, 560.

"THE CONSTITUTION IS AN EXPERIMENT!' AND 'WHILE THAT EXPERIMENT IS PART OF OUR SYSTEM."[79]

Holmes and Wigmore were old friends. Their friendship was probably the reason Wigmore did not refer to the two dissenters by name.[80] Indeed, a few years earlier, Wigmore had written a worshipful article titled "Justice Holmes and the Law of Torts."[81] Wigmore began:

> As I look over the long list of judges of American Supreme Courts, ... Justice Holmes seems to me the only one who has framed for himself a system of legal ideas and general truths of life and composed his opinions in harmony with the system already framed. ... [listing numerous commentators] — none of these (not to mention living ones) give the impression of having worked out, themselves, and for their own use, an harmonious construction of general principles.

Continuing, Wigmore added:

> Another trait of his opinions, and one that adds to their fascination, is the epigram instinct, which will not be suppressed ... No doubt, as a stylist, he is unique and unapproached ... Another commanding thing is the philosophy of life at large which decorates and dignifies his technical lore of the law .... Still another trait of his

---

[79] *Ibid.*, 561.
[80] Howe (ed.), *Holmes-Laski Letters*, I, 477, n. 1.
[81] 29 *Harvard Law Review* 601 (1915–1916).

opinions, of course, is the instinct for the history of the law. He cannot employ and apply a principle without thinking of it as having a history....[82]

Holmes, said Wigmore, used a "concise and crystallized style of historical allusion ... while avoiding the prosy prolixity of exegetic elaboration...."[83] The article continued in the same tone, quoting Holmes to the end.

It is difficult to reconcile such praise with Wigmore's denunciation of Holmes's *Abrams* dissent. The only obvious distinction is that they deal with entirely different subjects, the 1915–1916 law review article with torts, the 1920 article with speech during wartime. Wigmore was and considered himself an objective scholar, certainly in the law of torts. But his rant in the speech article, in tone if not substance, is irreconcilable with his earlier article.

Holmes shrugged it off. He wrote to Pollock: "Wigmore, in the *Ill. Law Rev.* goes for me *ex cathedra* as to my dissent in the *Abrams case*. You didn't agree with it, but Wigmore's explosion struck me, (I only glanced at it), as sentiment rather than reasoning — and in short, I thought it bosh. He has grown rather dogmatic in tone, with success...."[84]

Holmes's statement that Pollock "didn't agree" with his *Abrams* dissent referred to a letter from Pollock to Holmes on December 1, 1919, complaining that, "I don't see why there

---

[82] *Ibid.*, 601–604.
[83] *Ibid.*, 605.
[84] Mark DeWolfe Howe (ed.), *Holmes-Pollock Letters: The Correspondence of Mr. Justice Holmes and Sir Frederick Pollock, 1874–1932* 2nd edition (Cambridge, Massachusetts, 1961), II, 42, April 25, 1920.

was not evidence to go to the jury on the fourth count" in *Abrams*. That count charged conspiracy to "advocate curtailment of production of things and products, to wit, ordnance and ammunition, necessary and essential to the prosecution of the war." There were two reasons, as Holmes had plainly explained in his *Abrams* dissent. First, the requisite intent had not been proved because the defendants' complaints could have been made legitimately by a "patriot" who believed that money was being spent unnecessarily on certain products like "aeroplanes or cannons." The second reason was that the defendants were preaching their own creed which, Holmes believed, "no one has a right even to consider" under the First Amendment.[85]

Pollock also said in his December 1, 1919 letter: "It puzzles me also, I confess, that a special act of Congress should be necessary to make seditious denunciation of the Government and incitements to rebellion, in time of war, offences of some kind."[86] This "confession" appears to explain the reason for Pollock's objection to the *Abrams* dissent. Holmes thought so, because in his next letter he pointed out that, "As to the *Abrams* case, your puzzle as to a special act of Congress being necessary is answered by the consideration that there are *no crimes* against the U.S. except *by statute*."[87] In short, there are no common law crimes in the U.S. at any level of government.

---

[85] *Abrams v. U.S., supra*, 617.
[86] Howe (ed.), *Holmes-Pollock Letters*, II, 31.
[87] *Ibid.*, 32, emphasis added.

Holmes went on to say to Pollock, "I think it possible that I was wrong in thinking that there was no evidence of the Fourth Count in consequence of my attention being absorbed by the two leaflets that were set forth. But I still am of opinion that I was right, if I am right in what I devoutly believe, that an actual intent to hinder the U.S. in its war *with Germany* must be proved."[88] He said, "[I]t seems to me plain that the only object of the leaflets was to hinder our interference with Russia [an act not charged]. I ought to have developed this in the opinion. But that is ancient history now."[89]

It is remarkable that the author of an opinion which is arguably one of the best ever written by an American judge would say he might have done it better. Holmes was being humble here with little reason for humility. In fact, he had emphasized in his *Abrams* dissent that very point. As he wrote, the *Abrams* defendants intended to *help Russia* and stop American intervention there against the popular government — not to impede the United States in the war it was carrying on against Germany.[90]

Holmes did not hold a grudge over Wigmore's article attacking him. In 1923, at Wigmore's request, Holmes contributed an Introduction to the first volume of Wigmore's *The Modern Legal Philosophy Series*, which Holmes referred to in a letter to Laski — possibly tongue in cheek — as "one of Wigmore's enlightening collections."[91]

---

[88] *Ibid.*, emphasis in original.
[89] *Ibid.*
[90] *Abrams v. U.S., supra*, 629.
[91] Howe (ed.), *Holmes-Laski Letters*, I, 477 (Feb. 5, 1923).

Holmes's *Abrams* dissent represents an example of his ability to detach his personal views from his judicial opinions. The defendants in *Abrams* were communists who espoused the cause of the Russian Revolution. Holmes personally loathed communism. But he was able to define the protection of the First Amendment to include "the expression of opinions that we loathe...."[92]

And speaking of "opinions that we loathe," Holmes knew that Laski was a socialist. In several letters Holmes mentioned to Laski his disagreement with both Marxism and socialism. Indeed all "isms" were off limits in Holmes's mind. Holmes said Hegel could not make him "believe a syllogism could wag its tail." Hegel, he said, made "misty word poems in the form of syllogisms."[93] Holmes had no belief in the "importance of man," and found "no reason to believe a shudder would go through the sky if the whole antheap were kerosened."[94] Holmes thought Marx "treats ownership and consumption as convertible terms."[95] He meant Marx advocated that ownership and consumption should be the same for all citizens. Laski may have agreed with Marx's proposition. Holmes wrote Laski several times on this subject, candidly but gently expressing his disagreement with Laski's socialist views. He told Laski:

> I don't sympathize very greatly with your dream ... I think I perceive ... a tacit assumption that papa Laski, or those

---

[92] *Abrams v. U.S., supra*, 630.
[93] Howe (ed.), *Holmes-Laski Letters*, I, 350–351.
[94] *Ibid.*
[95] *Ibid.*, 410.

who think like him, are to regulate the popular desires ... As to the *right* of citizens to support and education, I don't see it. It may be a desirable idea to aim at, but I see no *right* in my neighbor to share my bread. I mean *moral right* of course. I have always said the rights of a given crowd are what they will fight for.[96]

Addressing a book by Laski on socialism, Holmes said, "I am worried" about it. "I don't agree with your premises and I must add that the *elaborate construction of an imaginary society* seems to me premature and like the constitution makers of the 18th century... I take no stock in abstract rights, I equally fail to respect the passion for equality ... which culminates in the statement of one of your Frenchmen that *inequality of talents was an injustice.*"[97] Then, with characteristic kindness, he said, "I hope I have not hurt my friend."

Discussions in correspondence with Laski included a question by Laski: Where did Holmes's ideas in his book *The Common Law* come from? Holmes said he "went through much anguish of mind" before he had an answer, and "I rooted around and made notes *until the theory emerged.*"[98]

Holmes used correspondence with friends to develop thoughts on a wide variety of subjects. For instance, he wrote to Laski, "There is a tendency to think of judges as if they were independent mouthpieces of the infinite, and not just *directors of a force* that comes from the source that *gives them the authority....* I have said that the Common Law isn't a

---

[96] Howe (ed.), *Holmes-Laski Letters*, I, 761–762, emphasis added.
[97] *Ibid.*, 768–769, emphasis added.
[98] *Ibid.*, 429–430, emphasis added.

brooding omnipresence in the sky and that the U.S. is not subject to some *mystic overlaw* that it is bound to obey."[99]

After the four 1919 espionage decisions, cases coming to the Supreme Court took a different shape than had the Espionage Act prosecutions. But they continued to involve statutes that punished speech, the Court continued to affirm convictions, and Holmes continued to dissent.

In *Gitlow v. New York*,[100] Gitlow was convicted and sentenced to prison for violating a New York statute punishing "criminal anarchy," which the statute defined as advocacy of "the doctrine that organized government should be overthrown by force, violence, assassination of public officials," among other acts. Gitlow was a member of the Left Wing Section of the Socialist Party that rejected the "dominant policy of 'moderate Socialism.'" A conference of this Section adopted a "Left Wing Manifesto," and a "Communist Program" that was published in the official organ of the party. Gitlow was on the board of managers of the paper and its business manager. He was involved in having 16,000 copies printed. The Court made clear that, "There was no evidence of any effect resulting from the publication and circulation of the Manifesto."[101] The Court pointed out that Gitlow's counsel had asked the trial judge to include in his instructions to the jury that to constitute criminal anarchy "it was necessary that the language used or published should advocate, teach or advise the duty, necessity

---

[99] Howe (ed.), *Holmes-Laski Letters*, II, 896, emphasis added.
[100] 268 U.S. 652 (1925).
[101] *Ibid.*, 655.

or propriety of doing 'some definite or immediate act or acts' of force, violence or unlawfulness directed toward the overthrowing of organized government.'"[102] The trial judge denied the request.

The denial is puzzling. The language "some definite or immediate act or acts," or similar language, would appear to be necessary to convey the clarity and immediacy demanded by the clear-and-present danger test.

Nevertheless, the Court said that the only question was whether the words published violated the Constitution, assuming that freedom of speech and of the press are among the personal rights and liberties protected by the due process clause of the 14th Amendment from impairment by the States.[103] The majority affirmed the convictions, holding that the New York statute "does not penalize the utterance or publication of abstract 'doctrine' or academic discussion having no quality of incitement to any concrete action ... What it prohibits is language advocating, advising or teaching the overthrow of organized government by unlawful means. These words imply urging action ... and necessarily imply the use of force and violence."[104] The words "by their very nature, involve danger to the public peace and to the security of the State," and are an "immediate danger."[105]

Holmes dissented, joined by Brandeis. The dissent was contained in two paragraphs. Holmes invoked the clear-and-present danger test, adopted by the full Court in *Schenck v.*

---

[102] *Ibid.*, 661.
[103] *Ibid.*, 666.
[104] *Ibid.*
[105] *Ibid.*

United States, and said that, "If what I think the correct test is applied, it is manifest that there was no present danger of an attempt to overthrow the government by force...."[106]

Continuing, Holmes wrote:

> It is said that this manifesto was more ... than a theory, that it was an incitement. Every idea is an incitement. It offers itself for belief and if believed it is acted on unless some other belief outweighs it or some failure of energy stifles the movement at its birth.... Eloquence may set fire to reason. But whatever may be thought of the redundant discourse before us it had no chance of starting a present conflagration. If in the long run the beliefs expressed in proletarian dictatorship are destined to be accepted by the dominant forces of the community, the only meaning of free speech is that they shall be given their chance and have their way.[107]

This dissent again displayed Holmes's remarkable ability to separate his legal rulings from his personal views. As we have seen, Holmes despised socialism and communism, along with all other "isms." Yet he was willing as a judge to allow speech urging a "proletarian dictatorship" if the "dominant forces" accept it.

Holmes wrote his final dissent in a speech case shortly after his 88th birthday, in *United States v. Schwimmer*.[108] Rosika Schwimmer, born in 1877 and a citizen of Hungary,

---

[106] *Ibid.*, 671.
[107] *Ibid.*
[108] 279 U.S. 644 (1929).

SPEECH

came to the United States in August 1921 to visit and lecture. She was a well-educated linguist, lecturer, and writer. In 1926 she filed a petition for naturalization. "On a preliminary form, she stated that she understood the principles of and fully believed in our form of government and that she had read, and was willing to take, the oath of allegiance."[109] Question 22 on the application asked, "If necessary, are you willing to take up arms in defense of this country?" She answered, "I would not take up arms personally." She stated, in correspondence, that "I am an uncompromising pacifist." She said, "Highly as I prize the privilege of American citizenship I could not compromise my way into it by giving an untrue answer to question 22 [on the application form], though for all practical purposes I might have done so, as even men of my age — I was 49 years old last September — are not called upon to take up arms ...."[110]

The majority opinion held Schwimmer was not entitled to citizenship, stating that "Such persons [as pacifists] are liable to be incapable of the attachment for and devotion to the principles of our Constitution that is required of aliens seeking naturalization."[111]

Dissenting, with Justice Brandeis again joining, Holmes reached for the stars. He began:

> The applicant seems to be a woman of superior character and intelligence, obviously more than ordinarily desirable as a citizen of the United States .... And as to the opinion, the whole examination shows that she holds none of the now-

---

[109] *Ibid.*, 646–647.
[110] *Ibid.*, 649.
[111] *Ibid.*, 652.

dreaded creeds but thoroughly believes in organized government and prefers that of the United States to any others in the world. *Surely it cannot show lack of attachment to the principles of the Constitution that she thinks that it can be improved.* I suppose that most intelligent people think that it might be. Her particular improvement looking to the abolition of war seems to me not materially different in its bearing on this case from a wish to establish cabinet government as in England, or a single house, or one term of seven years for the President. To touch a more burning question, *only a judge mad with partisanship* would exclude because the applicant thought that the *Eighteenth Amendment* [prohibition] should be repealed.[112]

Holmes then moved to the issue of war.

Of course the fear is that if a war came the applicant would exert activities such as were dealt with in *Schenck* ... But that seems to me unfounded. Her position and motives are wholly different from those of Schenck. *She is an optimist* and states in strong and, I do not doubt, sincere words her belief that war will disappear and that the impending destiny of mankind is to unite in peaceful leagues. I do not share that optimism nor do I think that a philosophic view of the world would regard war as absurd. But *most people who have known it regard it with horror, as a last resort*...The notion that the applicant's optimistic anticipations would make her a worse citizen is sufficiently

---

[112] *Ibid.,* 653–654, emphasis added.

answered by her examination, which seems to me a better argument for her admission than any that I can offer.[113]

Holmes thought the very idea of freedom was at stake. Today his argument might be called "libertarian." He continued:

> Some of her answers might excite popular prejudice, but if there is any principle of the Constitution that more imperatively calls for attachment than any other it is the principle of free thought — *not free thought for those who agree with us but freedom for the thought that we hate.* I think that we should adhere to that principle with regard to admission into, as well as to life within this country. And recurring to the opinion that bars this applicant's way, I would suggest that the Quakers have done their share to make the country what it is, that many citizens agree with the applicant's belief *and that I had not supposed hitherto that we regretted our inability to expel them because they believe more than some of us do in the teachings of the Sermon on the Mount.*[114]

Anthony Lewis, the distinguished journalist, author, and First Amendment scholar, said that in reading Holmes's dissent, "When I came to the final paragraph, ending ... 'sermon on the Mount,' I felt the hair rise on the back of my neck."[115]

After reading Holmes's dissent, Rosika Schwimmer wrote to him to express her "deep-felt" gratitude for his dissent, which had "helped [her] to take the blow of refusal without

---

[113] *Ibid.,* 654, emphasis added.
[114] *Ibid.,* 654–655, emphasis added.
[115] Lewis, *Freedom for the Thought That We Hate,* 33, 37–38.

loss of faith in the inherent idealism of your nation."[116] Holmes responded with his own letter, first protesting that in writing his opinion he was simply doing his duty, then continued, "... I must add that of course I am gratified by your more than kind expression."[117]

One writer asserts that Holmes's dissenting opinions in *Abrams* and *Schwimmer* were "inconsistent." This theory assumes that Holmes's 1919 dissent in *Abrams* — stating that "the best test of truth is the power of the thought to get itself accepted in the competition of the market" — is a "majoritarian" justification for speech because it invokes the market, thus a majority. In contrast, this theory claims, Holmes's 1929 dissent in *Schwimmer* was "openly counter majoritarian" because the speech it protects is freedom to express "the thought that we hate."[118]

This supposed inconsistency is a phantom. It ignores Holmes's language in *Abrams* that, "[W]e should be eternally vigilant against attempts to check the expression of *opinions that we loathe* ...."[119] Holmes's view expressed in his *Schwimmer* dissent is identical to the thought expressed in *Abrams*, both invoking "freedom for the thought that we hate" (*Schwimmer*) or "loathe" (*Abrams*).

Holmes's 1927 decision in *Buck v. Bell*,[120] has engendered the most criticism.[121] Writing for an eight-member majority,

---

[116] Baker, *The Justice from Beacon Hill*, 625.
[117] *Ibid.*, 626.
[118] White, *Justice Oliver Wendell Holmes*, 450–451.
[119] *Abrams v. U.S., supra*, 630, emphasis added.
[120] 274 U.S. 200 (1927).

Holmes's opinion upheld a 1924 Virginia statute that allowed the sterilization of "mental defectives" who were confined to state mental institutions. Holmes emphasized the procedural safeguards afforded patients who were considered for sterilization. These included notice to the inmates, the right to produce evidence, a hearing before a board of directors, written findings, and the right to appeal to a local court, all assuring the inmate was afforded due process of law. Holmes wrote that sterilization could be done without detriment to the inmate's general health.[122] Obviously, said Holmes, "we cannot say as matter of law" that grounds for sterilization "do not exist."[123] He concluded, with the often-quoted statement, "Three generations of imbeciles are enough."[124]

Chief Justice William Howard Taft, assigning the case to Holmes, wrote him a note suggesting that he "make a little full the care Virginia has taken in guarding against undue or hasty action, the proven absence of danger to the patient, and any other circumstances tending to lessen the shock that many feel over such a remedy." Continuing, Taft said, "The strength of the facts in three generations of course is the strongest argument for the necessity for state action and its reasonableness."[125]

---

[121] See David Oshinsky, "No Justice for the Weak," *New York Times* Book Review, March 20, 2016, p. BR1, for a review of two books, one speculating about what Holmes "wanted to hear" regarding Carrie Buck.
[122] *Buck v. Bell, supra*, 207.
[123] *Ibid.*
[124] *Ibid.*
[125] White, *Justice Oliver Wendell Holmes*, 404.

The eight-member majority included Justices Louis D. Brandeis and Harlan Fiske Stone. Justice Owen J. Roberts dissented but without opinion.

Seen in retrospect, the practice of compulsory sterilization seems harsh. But when Holmes wrote his opinion, it was considered enlightened, a way of producing a better society.[126] For example, one report states that California adopted a compulsory sterilization law in 1909 and did not repeal it until 1979, after thousands of people had been sterilized.[127]

An understanding of the historical context that existed when *Buck* was decided contributes to an appreciation of the decision and the social climate in which it grew. During a period that was called the Progressive Era — from roughly the 1890's to the 1920's — there was a broad public consensus that government should be the primary agent for change. Idealistic followers of the movement adopted new legislation that included minimum-wage and maximum-hours, antitrust laws, appropriations for roads and bridges, efforts to stamp out alcohol and prostitution.

But, paradoxically, the era also spawned sometimes well-intentioned white leaders' "reforms" of "others," which some historians characterize as manipulation of "lesser" people.[128]

---

[126] *Ibid.*, 407.

[127] *See* Mark G. Bold, "Our Debt on Sterilization," *Los Angeles Times*, March 6, 2015, p. A17.

[128] Gary Gerstle, *American Crucible: Race and Nation in the Twentieth Century* (Princeton, New Jersey, 2001), addresses this view throughout the book; *see also*, Adam Cohen, "Harvard's Eugenics Era: When academics embraced scientific racism, immigration restrictions, and the suppression of the 'unfit,'" *Harvard Magazine*, March-April 2016, pp. 48–52.

Federal government policy toward Native Americans tried assimilating them as farmers by allotting individual land plots and sending their children to boarding schools to learn English and Christianity. Congress aimed immigration restriction laws against southern and eastern Europeans, as well as Asians, partly to protect organized labor. Even Louis Brandeis's famous "Brandeis Brief," in *Muller v. Oregon* which, in 1908, helped Oregon laundresses escape workdays longer than 10 hours, would likely rub 21st-century female progressives the wrong way. One summary of Brandeis's argument said: "The reasons for the reduction of the working day to ten hours — (a) the physical organization of women, (b) her maternal functions, (c) the rearing and education of the children, (d) the maintenance of the home — ... need hardly be discussed."[129]

Just as *Buck v. Bell* strikes us today as harsh, it is of a piece with what white progressives saw as enlightened attitudes and laws on race. On March 21, 1915, in the White House, President Woodrow Wilson screened and praised D.W. Griffith's blockbuster film *The Birth of a Nation* which glorified the Ku Klux Klan as saviors from African Americans corrupted and manipulated by carpetbaggers, and was based on Wilson's good friend Thomas Dixon's novel *The Clansman*.

---

[129] Tom Holm, *The Great Confusion in Indian Affairs: Native Americans and Whites in the Progressive Era* (Austin, Texas, 2005); www.ehow.com/info_8753580_immigrant-restrictions-during-progressive-era.html; www.pbs.org/wnet/supremecourt/capitalism/sources_document7/html.

White southern progressives passed state laws disenfranchising black voters as a "reform" against whites manipulating black voters for their own purposes.[130]

By 2015, a century later, Princeton University students were demanding that its trustees remove President Wilson's name from the campus in light of what they saw as Wilson's serial racism.[131]

In reporting on this imbroglio about Wilson's legacy, *The New York Times* of November 30, 2015 mentioned the counter-intuitive facts that both Jim Crow segregation and eugenics were themselves Progressive Era reforms.[132]

The notorious 1896 case *Plessy v. Ferguson*[133] applied the "separate but equal" doctrine to uphold a Louisiana statute forbidding railroads from selling first-class tickets to blacks in public accommodations. Numerous similar statutes followed, segregating streetcars in 1905, train depots and restaurants in 1906, textile plants in 1915–1916, circuses in 1917, pool halls in 1924, and beaches in 1934. Progressives saw such measures as reducing racial tensions, and therefore as felicitous "reforms."[134]

In light of all these "reforms," *Buck v. Bell* "posed no particular problems for progressives: the eugenics movement,

---

[130] David W. Southern, *The Progressive Era and Race: Reaction and Reform* (Wheeling, West Virginia, 2005), 97ff.

[131] "The Case Against Woodrow Wilson," *The New York Times* editorial board, November 25, 2015, A26.

[132] Jennifer Schuessler, "Woodrow Wilson's Legacy Gets Complicated," *The New York Times*, November 30, 2015.

[133] 163 U.S. 537 (1896).

[134] Damon Root, "When Bigots Become Reformers: The Progressive Era's Shameful Record on Race," reason.com/archives/2006/05/05when-bigots-become-reformers.

after all, was thought to be another of the social 'experiments' responsive to a modernizing America."[135] "At the peak of its popularity," writes Lynne Olson, "eugenics was promoted by governments, treated as a legitimate academic discipline by prestigious universities, and supported by influential individuals, among them Theodore Roosevelt, Woodrow Wilson, H.G. Wells, George Bernard Shaw, and John Maynard Keynes." Racist theories were also part of the culture in the U.S. military, even included in the mandatory reading at West Point and other institutions of higher learning.[136]

Addressing the attitude of progressives regarding eugenics, which is a present-day criticism of *Buck*, the legal scholar Judge Richard A. Posner, pointed out, "We should remember that belief in human eugenics was a staple of progressive thought in Holmes's lifetime; for example, it was one of the motivations behind the Planned Parenthood movement," supporting birth control.[137] Judge Posner, with undisguised admiration for Holmes, said, "Holmes should satisfy Hamlet's description of his father: 'He was a man, take him for all in all,/I shall not look upon his like again.'" Holmes, said Judge Posner, "wasn't perfect; he was only great. His massive distinction has not been dented by his many detractors."[138]

Years later, in *Skinner v. Oklahoma*,[139] the Supreme Court held violative of the 14th Amendment equal protection clause

---

[135] White, *Justice Oliver Wendell Holmes*, 408.
[136] Olson, *Those Angry Days*, 72–73; Joseph Bendersky, *The "Jewish Threat": The Anti-Semitic Politics of the U.S. Army* (New York, 2000), 28–29.
[137] Posner (ed.), *The Essential Holmes*, xxvii.
[138] *Ibid.*, xxix–xxx.
[139] 316 U.S. 535 (1942).

an Oklahoma statute requiring compulsory sterilization of "habitual criminals," which the statute defined as persons convicted of two or more "felonies involving moral turpitude."[140] The Court found that the statute invidiously discriminated between crimes of the "same quality of offense and sterilizes one and not the other."[141] The Court noted that *Buck v. Bell* was distinguishable because there sterilization was required to "enable those who otherwise must be kept confined to be returned to the world."[142] In *Skinner*, said the Court, "there is no such saving feature."[143] The Court then found that if a classification, such as the one in the Oklahoma statute, was allowed to pass constitutional muster, "distinctions which are 'very largely dependent upon history for explanation'[144] could readily become a rule of human genetics." Citing this passage from Holmes's book implies approval of his reference to the basis for common-law distinctions which are based on history.

As seen, Justice Stone had concurred with Holmes's opinion in *Buck*. In 1942, Stone, now Chief Justice, wrote an opinion concurring with the majority in *Skinner*, noting, "Undoubtedly a state may, after appropriate inquiry, constitutionally interfere with the personal liberty of the individual to prevent the transmission by inheritance of his socially injurious tendencies," citing *Buck*. Further, said Stone, "Science has found, and the law has recognized, that

---

[140] *Ibid.*, 536.
[141] *Ibid.*, 541.
[142] *Ibid.*, 542.
[143] *Ibid.*
[144] Holmes, *The Common Law*, 73.

there are types of mental deficiency associated with delinquency which are inheritable," but the law may not sweep within its scope "any class of habitual offenders ...."[145]

Thus, it is easy to construe ancient opinions through the lens of contemporary views of morality and propriety. What is difficult is to think of those decisions in terms of the standards then existent.

As mentioned, in writing for the court in *Buck*, Holmes had followed Chief Justice Taft's advice in emphasizing the care Virginia had taken to avoid making hasty decisions in ordering sterilization. Holmes's great respect for Taft was evident then and on many other occasions. When Taft was forced by poor health to resign from the Court on February 3, 1930, Holmes wrote to Taft a week later on behalf of himself and the other justices.

> We call you Chief Justice still, for we cannot give up the title by which we have known you all these later years and which you have made so dear to us ... you showed us in new form your voluminous capacity for getting work done, your humor that smoothed the tough places, your golden heart brought you love from every side and most of all from your brethren whose tasks you made happy and light.[146]

On June 3, 1929, Holmes received a letter from Susan Brandeis, the daughter of Justice Louis Brandeis. First she apologized for burdening Holmes with another letter, saying

---

[145] *Skinner v. Oklahoma, supra,* 542.
[146] Doris Kearns Goodwin, *The Bully Pulpit: Theodore Roosevelt, William Howard Taft, and the Golden Age of Journalism* (New York, 2013), 749, 866n.

she would not have written "had I not Father's implied assurance that this letter would be received but not answered." She said, "I am impelled by a desire to express my admiration of your dissent in the Schwimmer case." She said she had become an "ardent pacifist" after meeting with Rosika Schwimmer years earlier and hoped her grandchildren might see pacifism as the "law of the land." Closing, she said "I could not refrain from an expression of my admiration to you — the writer of this 'great dissent.'"[147]

The letter is representative of the way many of Holmes's decisions touched the hearts of his readers even when, as in his *Schwimmer* dissent, he personally disagreed with the views expressed.

Further, Holmes's *Schwimmer* dissent is an example of how eloquence of expression, combined with logical thought and concise language, may become substantive law. How can this happen? Holmes himself told us in his dissent in *Gitlow v. New York*. As we have seen, Holmes dissented from a decision upholding a conviction of Gitlow under New York's criminal anarchy statute for publishing "Manifestos" of the Socialist Party advocating overthrow of the U.S. government. The majority's holding that the Manifestos were a "direct incitement" of violence, not protected speech under the First Amendment, was challenged by Holmes's famous dissent which, in a few words, expressed thoughts that endure today. He told us that "[e]very idea is an incitement, [which] offers itself for belief...," and "If in the long run the beliefs

---

[147] *Louis Dembitz Brandeis: A Life Well Spent*, A Commemorative Exhibition at The Harvard Law School (1994).

expressed in proletarian dictatorship are destined to be accepted by the dominant forces of the community, the only meaning of free speech is that they should be given their chance and have their way."[148]

Suppose Holmes had not dissented, that he had not written separately, but had merely concurred with the words and holding of the Court in *Gitlow* or *Schwimmer*.[149] Who would remember the cases today? The "ideas" in the majority opinions have "offered themselves for belief" and have been noticed only by *their association with dissenting opinions*.

Holmes had a way of universalizing his ideas. "Every idea is an incitement" (*Gitlow*). "I suppose that most intelligent people think that [the Constitution] might be" improved (*Schwimmer*). "Most people who have known [war] regard it with horror." (*Schwimmer*). There are numerous other examples. In this way, Holmes entered a kind of intellectual partnership with his readers. Arm in arm, they moved to the measure of Holmes's thought.

Another characteristic of Holmes's thought might be called "reverse logic." Most opinions of judges give reasons they think their conclusions are right. In contrast, Holmes would often reverse that kind of reasoning. An example is his statement in *Schwimmer* about Quakers. He said, "... I had not supposed hitherto that we regretted our inability to expel them because they believe more than some of us do in the teachings of the Sermon on the Mount." In his *Abrams* dissent he wrote, "Persecution for the expression of opinions

---

[148] *Gitlow v. U.S., supra*, 673.
[149] *United States v. Schwimmer*, 279 U.S. at 654–655.

seems to me to be perfectly logical," while cautioning that "time has upset many fighting faiths ...."[150]

A further dimension of Holmes's opinions was his extraordinary ability as a maker of memorable phrases concisely summing up his thought. Consider: "Clear and present danger;" "[F]alsely shouting fire in a crowded theater;" "the marketplace of ideas;" "Great cases, like hard cases, make bad law;" "The Fourteenth Amendment does not enact Mr. Herbert Spencer's *Social Statics*;" "Freedom for the thought that we hate;" "A word is not a crystal, transparent and unchanged; it is the skin of a living thought and may vary greatly in color and content according to the circumstances and the time in which it is used."[151] There are countless other examples, but these will suffice to make the point.

Where did this brand of eloquence begin? It came from a man who was an omnivorous reader, who loved life in a natural way: observant and inquisitive; spending boyhood summers in the Berkshires; finding rocks that may have crystals in them, and especially granite which he loved as a boy; observing frogs and snakes and toads, who have had skins from Homer's day, to Emerson's, to Longfellow's, and Thoreau's Walden Pond. When Holmes sat down to write an

---

[150] *Abrams v. U.S., supra,* 630.
[151] *Towne v. Eisner, supra,* 418, 425: (Construing the meaning of words in the Income Tax Law, holding stock issued to shareholders was not income to them).

Holmesdale, Pittsfield, Massachusetts, c. 1905–1915.
(*Courtesy of Library of Congress*)

opinion, he brought to bear his whole life's experience, from catching tadpoles in 1849 to 1856 near Pittsfield, to climbing in the Swiss Alps with Leslie Stephen in 1866, to delighting in springtime flowers in Washington during his 1930's dotage, filtered through layers and layers of reading and writing dozens of speeches and hundreds of letters, all coming together in a "crystal ... skin ...."

Holmes's old friend Learned Hand related a conversation he had with Holmes who was Hand's judicial idol. On this occasion, when Holmes was about ninety, he told Hand that when he felt as though life did not seem worthwhile, "... I have an imaginary talk with the Great Panjandrum, who says to me, 'Well, Wendell, if that's how you feel, I can arrange it. How about tonight?' And then I always know that I should answer, 'Boss, could you just as well put that off a fortnight?'"[152]

---

[152] Gunther, *Learned Hand*, 675.

Holmes on his 89th birthday.
[Washington, DC: *Times Wide World*, March 8, 1930].
(*Courtesy of The Lawbook Exchange, Ltd.*)

12

Conclusion

On March 8, 1931, Holmes turned 90. A *Wall Street Journal* reporter noted: "By then the seemingly ageless judge was widely regarded as a national treasure, so CBS radio marked the occasion with a prime-time birthday tribute in which he spoke briefly from his home in Washington. Justice Holmes was the most eloquent jurist this country has yet produced, and he rose to the near-final occasion ...."[1]

Holmes said:

The riders in the race do not stop short when they reach the goal. There is a little finishing canter before coming to a standstill. There is time to hear the kind voice of friends and to say to oneself: The work is done. But just as one says that, the answer comes: The race is over, but the work never is done while the power to work remains.[2]

Closing, Holmes said:

For to live is to function. That is all there is to living. And so I end with a line from a Latin poet who uttered the

---

[1] Terry Teachout, "Voices from the Grave," *Wall Street Journal*, October 9, 2015.
[2] Mark DeWolfe Howe (comp.), *The Occasional Speeches of Justice Oliver Wendell Holmes* (Cambridge, Massachusetts, 1962), 178; White, *Justice Oliver Wendell Holmes,* 463–464, 586n.

message more than fifteen hundred years ago: "Death plucks my ears and says, "Live – I am coming.""

Holmes retired from the bench ten months later. As seen, Justice Harlan Fiske Stone served on the Court with Holmes and later became Chief Justice. On January 12, 1932, Stone wrote to Frankfurter:

> As you read your evening paper today, you will appreciate the feeling of sadness which has weighed upon me in the last few weeks, and especially since Sunday, when Justice Holmes concluded to terminate his long period of service on the bench . . . I asked Justice Holmes to ride with me for his last Court attendance. I found him in good spirits and treating the march of events in his true philosophical spirit. In this, as in everything else, he is the gallant gentleman, facing the future with equanimity and taking a just, although characteristically modest, pride in the past. I stopped for a little chat with him again tonight on the way down from Court and found him in good form. What a career of public service, and what a gallant, noble ending of it! Thus passed from the Court one of the greatest men who ever sat upon it, and one of the greatest men and most beautiful characters it has been my privilege to know.[3]

Holmes's closest friend on the Court was Justice Louis D. Brandeis, who was fifteen years younger than Holmes, and who had joined the Supreme Court in 1916. Brandeis had long known and admired Holmes. He was in the audience at

---

[3] Mason, *Harlan Fiske Stone*, 323.

Justices Oliver Wendell Holmes, Jr. and Louis Dembitz Brandeis.
(*Courtesy of Historical & Special Collections, Harvard Law School Library.*
Record ID: olvwork390179)

the Lowell Institute when Holmes delivered his famous lectures on the common law in 1880, thirty-six years before Brandeis took his seat on the Court.[4] The two men shared a deep affection for each other. They would often walk to and from court together. Once when Holmes had a cold and did not attend the weekly conference, Brandeis noted that it "seemed dreary without him."

During the Court's adjournments, Brandeis visited Holmes, who wrote, "I am richer after a talk with him."[5]

---

[4] Urofsky, *Brandeis*, 565–566.
[5] Mennel and Compston (eds.), *Holmes and Frankfurter: Their Correspondence, 1912-1934*, p. 236, February 15, 1929.

After Holmes retired, Brandeis would visit him at least once a week. Holmes's housekeeper recalled that when she told him Brandeis was on his way "he would get awfully excited." She would take Brandeis in the elevator to Holmes's library where Holmes was seated in his big chair. Though Holmes was frail, he "would lift himself up and he would smile broadly and say, 'My dear friend,' and the two of them would embrace."[6]

Holmes lived life to the fullest, right to the end. At Christmas, 1934, Frankfurter sent a telegram to Holmes, ending it with, "Confidentially, there ain't no Santa Claus." Holmes replied, "Of course there is a Santa Claus. Don't be sentimental. Merry Xmas."[7]

Shortly before he died — two days before his 94th birthday — Holmes wrote an introduction to a biography of Brandeis by Frankfurter. Of Brandeis, Holmes said, "In the moments of discouragement that we all pass through, he always had the happy word that lifts up one's heart. It comes from knowledge, experience, courage, and the high way in which he has always taken life."[8] In a note to Frankfurter, Brandeis's wife Alice Goldmark Brandeis commented on Holmes's statement, writing, "Justice Holmes' little word — so beautiful and moving — is the crowning point of it all."[9]

---

[6] Urofsky, *Brandeis*, 566.
[7] Mennel and Compston (eds.), *Holmes and Frankfurter: Their Correspondence, 1912-1934*, pp. 278-279.
[8] *Ibid.*, 270.
[9] *Ibid.*, 271.

Acknowledgments

The authors recognize and thank John Gorham Palfrey, former vice-dean at the Harvard Law School, currently Head of School at Phillips Academy Andover, and great-grandson of John Gorham Palfrey, Justice Holmes's friend and executor.

The authors also thank Lesley Schoenfeld, Public Services and Visual Collections Administrator at Harvard Law School Library, who spent hours assisting us in securing permissions and locating images in Harvard's Holmes Digital Suite, the Library of Congress, and elsewhere. She was immensely helpful in tracking down countless Holmes memorabilia, including his lunchbox, a favorite desk and chair, portraits by Sally Tate and Charles Sydney Hopkinson, Holmes's death mask, and a thorough but elusive search for Holmes's bloody Civil War uniform and musket ball mentioned by biographer G. Edward White.

In addition, special acknowledgment goes to Eric Frazier, Rare Books & Special Collections reference librarian at the Library of Congress. Mr. Frazier gave us full access to two large rooms, upstairs on "Mahogany Row" facing the Capitol, and filled with a substantial portion of Justice Holmes's eclectic, prolific, and treasured book collection from both Beverly Farms and his Washington residence at 1720 Eye Street. Mr. Frazier snapped dozens of photographs — and later refined them for our book — of this rare Holmes Collection.

For other assistance at different stages, we thank Skip Freeman, Don MacQuarrie, Mary Grant, Kathy Cooper, Terri McFadden, Ed Brown, Fay Salt, Melissa Dolan, Paige Roberts, Michael Barker, Alastair and Leslie Adam, and Paul Kalkstein.

We could not have completed this book without the invaluable assistance of Barrett R. L. Evans of Montecito, California.

We acknowledge Valerie Horowitz, our editor, whose guidance has been crucial to the completion of this book.

Finally, to borrow from the wit of the late, great historian of economic thought William J. Barber, "None of the above should be incriminated for the shortcomings of the final product."

John Gorham Palfrey, great-grandson of Holmes's executor John Gorham Palfrey in 1935, standing in Holmes's 2nd floor study (2014) at Beverly Farms.
(*Courtesy of the authors*)

BIBLIOGRAPHY

Abrams v. U.S. 250 U.S. 616 (1919).

Acheson, David C., et alia. *Among Friends: Personal Letters of Dean Acheson.* New York, 1980.

Adams, Henry. *The Education of Henry Adams.* Cambridge, Massachusetts, 1918.

Allis, Frederick S., Jr. *Youth from Every Quarter: A Bicentennial History of Phillips Academy, Andover.* Hanover, New Hampshire, 1979.

Alschuler, Albert W. *Law Without Values: The Life, Work, and Legacy of Justice Holmes.* Chicago, 2000.

Aquinas, Thomas. *Summa Theologica.* Translated by Fathers of the English Dominican Province. New York, 1947.

Baker, Liva. *The Justice from Beacon Hill: The Life and Times of Oliver Wendell Holmes.* New York, 1991.

Baltzer v. U.S. 248 U.S. 593 (1918).

Bander, Edward J., ed. *Justice Holmes Ex Cathedra.* Buffalo, 1991.

Barrett, Edward L., et alia. *Constitutional Law.* Brooklyn, 1963.

Bendersky, Joseph. *The "Jewish Threat": The Anti-Semitic Politics of the U.S. Army.* New York, 2000.

Berg, A. Scott. *Wilson.* New York, 2013.

Berlin, Isaiah. "A Message to the 21st Century." *New York Review of Books.* October 23, 2014.

Biddle, Francis. *Justice Holmes, Natural Law, and the Supreme Court.* New York, 1961.

Biddle, Francis. *Mr. Justice Holmes.* New York, 1946.

Blasi, Vincent. "Holmes and the Marketplace of Ideas." *The Supreme Court Review*, 1. 2004.

Bold, Mark G. "Our Debt on Sterilization." *Los Angeles Times*, p. A17. March 6, 2015.

Bowen, Catherine Drinker. *Yankee from Olympus: Justice Holmes and His Family.* Boston, 1944.

Buck v. Bell 274 U.S. 200 (1927).

Burns, James MacGregor. *Packing the Court: The Rise of Judicial Power and the Coming Crisis of the Supreme Court.* New York, 2009.

Burns, Ken. *The Civil War: A Film by Ken Burns.* September, 1990.

Burton, David H., ed. *Holmes-Sheehan Correspondence: Letters of Justice Oliver Wendell Holmes, Jr. and Canon Patrick Augustine Sheehan.* Revised edition. New York, 1993.

Butcher's Benevolent Association of New Orleans v. Crescent City Live-Stock Landing & Slaughterhouse Co. 83 U.S. (16 Wall.) 36 (1973). See Slaughterhouse Cases.

Cardozo, Benjamin N. *The Nature of the Judicial Process.* New York, 1921.

"The Case Against Woodrow Wilson." *The New York Times* editorial board, p. A26. November 25, 2015.

"CBS News Sunday Morning." Aired January 1, 2017.

Celebrate Boston. http://www.celebrateboston.com/culture/brahmin-ori gin.htm

Chafee, Zechariah. "Freedom of Speech in Wartime." *Harvard Law Review* 32. 1919.

Chafee, Zechariah Jr. *Free Speech in the United States.* Cambridge, 1941.

Chemerinsky, Erwin. *The Case Against the Supreme Court.* New York, 2014.

Chicago, Milwaukee and St. Paul Railroad v. Minnesota 134 U.S. 418 (1890).

Cohen, Adam. "Harvard's Eugenics Era: When academics embraces scientific racism, immigration restrictions, and the suppression of the 'unfit.'" *Harvard Magazine*, pp. 48–52. March–April 2016.

Cohen, Felix. "Holmes-Cohen Correspondence." *Journal of the History of Ideas* 9, pp. 3, 14–15. 1948.

Cohen, Henry. "Oliver Wendell Holmes, Jr.: Life and Philosophy." *The Federal Lawyer*, pp. 23–25. New York, New York Times. January 2004.

Cook, Franklin H. "History of Rate Determination under Due Process Clauses." *University of Chicago Law Review* 11, p. 297. 1944.

Davidson v. New Orleans 96 U.S. 97 (1878).

Debs v. U.S. 249 U.S. 211 (1919).

Felton, R. Todd. *A Journey into the Transcendentalists' New England.* Berkeley, 2006.

Fiechter, Frederick C., Jr. "The Preparation of an American Aristocrat." *New England Quarterly* 6, pp. 3–5. 1933.

Foote, Shelby. *The Civil War: A Narrative.* New York, 1958.

Frankfurter, Felix. "Constitutional Opinions of Justice Holmes." *Harvard Law Review* 29, pp. 683, 691. 1915–1916.

Frankfurter, Felix. *Felix Frankfurter Reminisces.* Harlan Phillips, ed., 1962.

Frankfurter, Felix. *Mr. Justice Holmes and the Supreme Court.* Revised edition. Cambridge, Massachusetts, 1961.

Freund, Ernst. "The Debs Case and Free Speech." *New Republic*, Vol. 19, Issue 235, p. 13. May 1919.

Frohwerk v. U.S. 249 U.S. 204 (1919).

Gerstle, Gary. *American Crucible: Race and Nation in the Twentieth Century.* Princeton, New Jersey, 2001.

Ginsburg, Douglas H. "Afterword." *University of Chicago Law Review*, Vol. 40, number 2. Winter 1973.

Gitlow v. New York 268 U.S. 652 (1925).

Goodwin, Doris Kearns. *The Bully Pulpit: Theodore Roosevelt, William Howard Taft, and the Golden Age of Journalism.* New York, 2013.

Gregory, Charles Oscar. *Labor and the Law.* New York, 1946.

Gunther, Gerald. *Learned Hand: The Man and the Judge.* Cambridge, Massachusetts, 1994.

Healy, Thomas. *The Great Dissent: How Oliver Wendell Holmes Changed His Mind — and Changed the History of Free Speech in America.* New York, 2013.

Holm, Tom. *The Great Confusion in Indian Affairs: Native Americans and Whites in the Progressive Era.* Austin, Texas, 2005.

Holmes, Justice Oliver Wendell. Justice Oliver Wendell Holmes to John C.H. Wu, Sept. 6, 1925, in "Some Unpublished Letters of Justice Holmes" (Reprinted from *T'ien Hsia Monthly*, December, 1935), p. 280. Oliver Wendell Holmes, Jr., Addenda, 1818–1978, Box 4, Folder 7. Courtesy of Historical & Special Collections, Harvard Law School Library. Available online at http://nrs.harvard.edu/urn-3:HLS.Libr:86 70632?n=17.

Holmes, Justice Oliver Wendell. "Natural Law." *Harvard Law Review* 32, p. 40 ff. 1918.

Holmes, Oliver Wendell. *The Works of Oliver Wendell Holmes.* Boston, 1892.

Holmes, Oliver Wendell, Jr. Autobiographical sketch for college album, July 2, 1861. Quoted in Frederick C. Fiechter, Jr., "The Preparation of an American Aristocrat." *New England Quar-terly* 6, pp. 3–5. 1933.

Holmes, Oliver Wendell, Jr. *The Common Law*. Revised edition. New York, 2004.

Holmes, Oliver Wendell, Jr. "Law and the Court." Speech to Harvard Law School Association of New York, pp. 98, 101–102. February 15, 1913. Cited in Felix Frankfurter, "Constitutional Opinions of Justice Holmes," *Harvard Law Review* 29 (1915–1916), pp. 683, 691.

Holmes, Oliver Wendell, Jr. "Memorial Day." Keene, New Hampshire, May 30, 1884. Cited in Mark DeWolfe Howe ed., *The Occasional Speeches of Justice Oliver Wendell Holmes* (Cambridge, Massachusetts, 1962), 4.

Holmes, Oliver Wendell, Jr. "The Path of the Law." *Harvard Law Review* 10, p. 457. 1897.

Holmes, Oliver Wendell, Jr. "The Profession of the Law." *Speeches*, pp. 22 ff. Boston, 1913.

Holmes, Oliver Wendell, Jr. "The Soldier's Faith." Speech delivered Memorial Day 1895 to Harvard seniors. Quoted in Max Lerner (ed.), *The Mind & Faith of Justice Holmes* (New York, 1943), 20–21.

Howe, Mark DeWolfe. *Justice Oliver Wendell Holmes*. Vol. I. *The Shaping Years: 1841–1870*. Cambridge, Massachusetts, 1957.

Howe, Mark DeWolfe. *Justice Oliver Wendell Holmes*. Vol. II. *The Proving Years: 1870–1882*. Cambridge, Massachusetts, 1963.

Howe, Mark DeWolfe, ed. *Holmes-Laski Letters: The Correspondence of Mr. Justice Holmes and Harold J. Laski, 1916–1935*. Cambridge, Massachusetts, 1953.

Howe, Mark Antony DeWolfe. *Holmes of the Breakfast Table*. Mamaroneck, New York, 1972.

Howe, Mark DeWolfe, ed. *Holmes-Pollock Letters: The Correspondence of Mr. Justice Holmes and Sir Frederick Pollock, 1874–1932*. 2nd edition. Two volumes in one. Cambridge, Massachusetts, 1961.

Howe, Mark DeWolfe, comp. *The Occasional Speeches of Justice Oliver Wendell Holmes*. Cambridge, Massachusetts, 1962.

Howe, Mark DeWolfe, ed. *Touched With Fire: Civil War Letters and Diary of Oliver Wendell Holmes, Jr.* Revised edition. New York, 2000.

Hurtado v. California 110 U.S. 516 (1883).

BIBLIOGRAPHY 179

Hylton, Wil S. "The Unbreakable Laura Hillenbrand." *The New York Times* Magazine, pp. 31–40. December 21, 2014.

Immigrant-restrictions-during-progressive-era. www.ehow.com/info_8753580_immigrant-restrictions-during-progressive-era.html

Internet Encyclopedia of Philosophy: A Peer-Reviewed Academic Source. "John Stuart Mill (1806–1873)." Biography section, http://www.iep.utm.edu/milljs.

James, Henry. *American Scene.* London, 1907.

Jourolmon, Leon, Jr. "The Life and Death of Smyth v. Ames." *Tennessee Law Review* 18, pp. 347, 663, 756. 1943–1945.

King v. Burwell 135 S. Ct. 2480, 192 L. Ed. 2nd 483, 83 U.S.L.W. 4541 (2015).

Lee, Evan Tsen. *Judicial Restraint in America: How the Ageless Wisdom of the Supreme Court Was Invented.* New York, 2011.

Lerner, Max, ed. *The Mind and Faith of Justice Holmes: His Speeches, Essays, Letters, and Judicial Opinions.* New York, 1943.

Lewis, Anthony. *Freedom for the Thought that We Hate: A Biography of the First Amendment.* New York, 2007.

Louchheim, Katie, ed. *The Making of the New Deal: The Insiders Speak.* Cambridge, Massachusetts, 1983.

Louis Dembitz Brandeis: A Life Well Spent. A Commemorative Exhibition at The Harvard Law School. 1994.

MacLeish, Archibald and E.F. Pritchard, Jr., eds. "Introduction," in *Law and Politics: Occasional Papers of Felix Frankfurter, 1913–1938.* New York, 1939.

Mason, Alpheus Thomas. *Harlan Fiske Stone: Pillar of the Law.* New York, 1956.

Masses Publishing Co. v. Patten 244 Fed. 535 (1917).

Masses Publishing Co. v. Patten 245 Fed. 102 (C.C.A. 2nd 1917).

McPherson, James M. *Battle Cry of Freedom: The Civil War Era.* New York, 1988.

McPherson, James M. "The Monstrous War." *New York Review of Books*, p. 69. July 10, 2014.

Mennel, Robert M., and Christine L. Compston, eds. *Holmes and Frankfurter: Their Correspondence, 1912–1934.* Durham, New Hampshire, 1996.

Monagan, John S. *The Grand Panjandrum: Mellow Years of Justice Holmes.* Lanham, Maryland, 1988.

Morse, John T., Jr. *Life and Letters of Oliver Wendell Holmes.* Boston, 1896.

Muller v. Oregon 208 U.S. 412 (1908).

Munn v. Illinois 94 U.S. 113 (1877).

National Federation of Independent Business v. Sebelius, 567 U.S. 519, 132 S. Ct. 2566, 183 L. Ed. 2d 450, 53 EBC 1513, 80 U.S.L.W. 4579 (2012).

Nevins, Allan. *Study in Power: John D. Rockefeller.* New York, 1953.

Northern Securities Co. v. U.S. 193 U.S. 197 (1904).

Novick, Sheldon, ed. *Collected Works of Justice Holmes: Complete Public Writings and Selected Judicial Opinions of Oliver Wendell Holmes.* Chicago, 1994.

Novick, Sheldon. "Justice Holmes and the Art of Biography." *William & Mary Law Review* 33, pp. 1219 ff. 1992.

Novick, Sheldon. "The Unrevised Holmes and Freedom of Expression." *The Supreme Court Review,* p. 304 ff. 1991.

Obergefell v. Hodges 135 S. Ct. 2584, 192 L.Ed. 2nd 609, 83 U.S.L.W. 4592 (2015).

Olson, Lynne. *Those Angry Days: Roosevelt, Lindbergh, and America's Fight over World War II, 1939–1945.* New York, 2013.

Oshinsky, David. "No Justice for the Weak." *New York Times* Book Review, p. BR1. March 20, 2016.

Parks, Tim. "Montaigne: What Was Truly Courageous?" *New York Review of Books,* Vol. LXII Number 18, p. 59. November 24, 2016.

Peabody, James E., ed. *Holmes-Einstein Letters.* New York, 1964.

Perkins, Rollin M. *Perkins on Criminal Law.* Brooklyn, 1957.

Petronella, Mary Melvin, ed. *Victorian Boston Today: Twelve Walking Tours.* Boston, 2004.

Plant v. Woods 176 Mass. 492 (1900).

Plessy v. Ferguson 163 U.S. 537 (1896).

Pollock v. Farmer's Loan and Trust Co. 157 U.S. 429 (1895).

Pound, Roscoe. "The world now moved to the measure of Holmes's thought." *Harvard Law Review* 35, p. 449. 1921.

Posner, Richard A., ed. *The Essential Holmes: Selections from the Letters, Speeches, Judicial Opinions, and Other Writings of Oliver Wendell Holmes, Jr.* Chicago, 1992.

BIBLIOGRAPHY

Posner, Richard A., and Eric J. Segall. "Scalia's Majoritarian Theocracy." *The New York Times*, p. A35. December 3, 2015.
Rawls, *A Theory of Justice*. Revised edition. Cambridge, Massachusetts, 1999.
Reagan v. Farmer's Loan and Trust. 154 U.S. 362 (1894).
Root, Damon. "When Bigots Become Reformers: The Progressive Era's Shameful Record on Race." reason.com/archives/2006/05/05when-bigots-become-reformers
Rosen, Jeffrey. "John Roberts, the Umpire in Chief." *The New York Times*, p. 4. June 28, 2015.
Savage, David G. "Chief Justice is Full of Surprises." *Los Angeles Times*, pp. A-1, 8. September 29, 2015.
Schenck v. U.S. 249 U.S. 47 (1919).
Schuessler, Jennifer. "Woodrow Wilson's Legacy Gets Complicated." *The New York Times*. November 30, 2015.
Skinner v. Oklahoma 316 U.S. 535 (1992).
Slaughterhouse Cases. See *Butcher's Benevolent Association of New Orleans v. Crescent City Live-Stock Landing & Slaughterhouse Co.* 83 U.S. (16 Wall.) 36 (1973).
Smyth v. Ames 169 U.S. 466 (1898).
Southern, David W. *The Progressive Era and Race: Reaction and Reform*. Wheeling, West Virginia, 2005.
Southern Pacific Co. v. Jensen. 244 U.S. 205 (1917).
Steele, Richard W. *Free Speech in the Good War*. New York, 1999.
Stevens, John Paul. *Five Chiefs: A Supreme Court Memoir*. New York, 2011.
Stewart, Matthew. *The Courtier and the Heretic: Leibniz, Spinoza, and the Fate of God in the Modern World*. New Haven, 2006.
Teachout, Terry. "Voices from the Grave." *Wall Street Journal*. October 9, 2015.
Towne v. Eisner 245 U.S. 418 (1918).
Twain, Mark (Samuel Clemens). *Life on the Mississippi*, in *Mississippi Writings*. 1883; reprint, New York, 1982.
United States v. Butler 297 U.S. 1 (1936).
United States v. Schwimmer 279 U.S. 644 (1929).
Updike, John. "Hub Bids Kid Adieu." *The New Yorker*. October 22, 1960.
Urofsky, Melvin I. *Louis D. Brandeis: A Life*. New York, 2009.

Vegelahn v. Guntner 167 Mass. 92 (1896).

West Coast Hotel Co. v. Parrish 300 U.S. 379 (1937).

White, G. Edward. *Justice Oliver Wendell Holmes: Law and the Inner Self.* New York, 1993.

Wigmore, John H. "Abrams v. U.S.: Freedom of Speech and Freedom of Thuggery in War-Time and Peace-Time." *Illinois Law Review*, XIV, p. 539. March, 1920.

Wigmore, John H. "Justice Holmes and the Law of Torts." *Harvard Law Review* 29, p. 601. 1915–1916.

Wister, Owen. *Roosevelt: The Story of a Friendship, 1880–1919.* New York, 1930.

Wolff, Tobias Barrington. "The Three Voices of Obergefell." *Los Angeles Lawyer*, p. 31. December 2015.

Wyzanski, Charles E., Jr. "The Democracy of Justice Oliver Wendell Holmes." *Vanderbilt Law Review* 7, p. 311 ff. 1954.

Wyzanski, Charles E., Jr. *Whereas: A Judge's Premises.* Boston, 1944.

INDEX

A

Abbott, Henry L. (son), 40, 46–47
Abbott, Josiah G. (father), 46
Abrams, Jacob, 128, 114, 142
Abrams v. U.S., 11, 129, 132, 134–136, 138, 140, 141, 145–148, 156, 166
Adams, Brooks, 32
Adams, Henry, 31
Adams, John, 22
Adams, Sam, 22
A.D. Club (Harvard College), 27, 31
Aeschylus, 76
Affordable Care Act (*see also*, Patient Protection and Affordable Care Act), 99, 111
Agricultural Adjustment Act, 80
alcohol, as target of progressives, 158
Alexander the Great, 30
Alexandrovich, Alexis (Grand Duke of Russia), 76
Alger, Horatio, 29
amendment in 1918 to the 1917 Espionage Act, 129
"anarchists," 129
Andover (Phillips Academy), 24
Annals of America (Abiel Holmes, 1800), 21–22, 56

Antietam Creek, Battle of, 42, 43, 43n., 49
antitrust laws, 79–80, 91, 95–99, 158
Anti-war Proclamation and Program, 120
Apologia (John Henry Newman), 74
appellate courts, 108, 131
appellate judge, role of, 108, 131
Aquinas, Thomas, St., 63, 68–69
Arnold, Matthew, 75
Athenaeum, Boston, 31, 34
Athens, Greece, 75
Atlantic Monthly, The, 25

B

"bad man" metaphor (Holmes, Jr.), 54, 55
Baker, Liva, 89
bakers, in *Lochner v. New York*, 104
Ball's Bluff, Battle of, 41
Baltzer v. U.S., Holmes's dissent favoring free speech in, 138–140
battles, Civil War, 26, 40–42, 43n., 44, 49
  Antietam Creek, 42, 43n., 49
  Ball's Bluff, 41
  Fredericksburg, 44
  Gettysburg, 40

Beacon Hill, 29, 48
Bentham, Jeremy, 19, 20, 75
Bergson, Henri, 76
Berkshires, 25, 30, 166
Bernouilli, Daniel, 75
Beveridge, Senator and Mrs. Albert J., 17
Beverly Farms, 2, 4–17, 70, 74, 76, 78–80, 174
Biddle, Francis, 17, 33, 60, 62–64
bill of rights, 139
Bill of Rights, to the U.S. Constitution, 68
biographers, of Oliver Wendell Holmes, Jr.,
   Francis Biddle, 33, 60, 62–64, 71
   G. Edward White, 156, 156n.
   John Monagan, 27
   Liva Baker, 89
   Mark DeWolfe Howe, 28, 80
Birth of a Nation, The (D.W. Griffith), 159
Blackstone, Sir William, 22
Bolsheviks, 141
Bonaparte, Napoleon, 55
books, as part of the "laboratory," 20, 25–26, 31, 34, 71–77
Boston Athenaeum, 31, 34
Boston State House ("hub of the solar system"), 29
Bradstreet, Anne, 21
Brahmin, Boston, 26, 28, 29, 29n., 30, 34, 98
Brandeis, Alice Goldmark (wife), 17, 172
"Brandeis Brief," 56, 159

Brandeis, Justice Louis Dembitz, 17, 55–56, 65–66, 97, 129–130, 138, 141, 152–153, 158–159, 164, 170–172
Brandeis, Susan (daughter), 164
"Breakfast Table" column (Holmes, Sr.), 25
Brewer, Justice David Josiah, 103, 105
"brooding omnipresence in the sky" (Holmes, Jr.), 53, 57, 64, 150
Buck v. Bell, 157–159, 161, 162–163
Bundy, Harvey, 17
Buzzards Bay (from 1874–1887 a summer home, Holmes, Jr., and Fanny), 33

C

Cabot family, 21
California gold rush, 30
California sterilization law, 158
"Can't Helps" (Holmes, Jr.), 64
Cardozo, Justice Benjamin N., 111
Case Against the Supreme Court, The, 83, 84n.
Cather, Willa, 73
Causeries (Charles Augustin Saint-Beuve), 76
CBS radio broadcast (farewell by Justice Holmes), 169
Chafee, Zechariah, 126–128, 135–136, 140
Chemerinsky, Erwin, 83, 84n.

INDEX

Chicago Law Review, University of, 123
Chicago, Milwaukee & St. Paul Railway Co. v. Minnesota, 102, 104
Child, Lydia, 29
Civil War, 26, 32, 33, 35, 36, 37ff., 91
Clansman, The (Thomas Dixon, author), 159
Clark, Justice John H., 129
"clear and present danger" (Justice Holmes), 117, 118, 121, 128, 130, 137n., 152, 166
"clericalism," 76
Cleveland, Ohio, 60
Cohen, Henry, 111–112, 112n.
combination in restraint of trade, 95–98
commerce clause, 96, 98
common law, 53, 146, 150, 162, 171
Common Law, The, 33, 50–53, 60, 69, 74, 86, 149
communism, 148, 152
"competition of the market," 134, 142, 143, 156
Comte, Auguste, 31
Congress, 80, 96, 98, 99, 111, 115, 117, 118, 131, 146, 159
constitutional right, 139
Constitution, U.S., "evolving," vs. "originalism," 87
contract, right of, 105
Corcoran, Thomas, 17
court-packing (FDR), 112
"criminal attempt," law of, 117

Croly, Herbert, 126
Cutting, Mrs. Bayard (Olivia Murray), 59

D

"dame's school "(nursery school), 30
Davidson v. New Orleans, 102
Davis, John W., 79
Debs, Eugene, 119ff, 123, 124–126, 128, 137, 140
Debs v. U.S., 119ff., 122, 123, 131–132, 135, 136, 137, 140
Declaration of Independence, 23, 64
Decline and Fall of the Roman Empire, The (Edward Gibbon), 72
Descartes, Rene, 54
Dewey, John, 77
Dickens, Charles, 29, 31
"direct advocacy," 124–125
Dixon, Thomas (*The Clansman*), 159
Dixwell, Epes S., 30
Dixwell, Fanny (maiden name, spouse of OWH, Jr.), 33
Dixwell's Latin School, 30
draft, the, 115–117, 120, 125, 133, 138
Doyle, Sir Arthur Conan, 29
due process clause, 101ff., 113, 157

E

E.C. Knight Co., 99
economic theory, judges and, 108
education of a child, 20
Eighteenth Amendment, 154
Election of 1912, 119
Eliot, George (Mary Anne Evans), 73
Emerson, Ralph Waldo, 29, 31, 72, 166
England, 32, 52–54, 154
English law, 52–53, 80
equal protection clause, 102, 112, 162
espionage, 120, 128, 130, 132, 139–140, 150
Espionage Act, 1917 (amended 1918), 115–116, 119, 120, 121, 123–124, 128, 130, 140, 150
espionage cases, 115ff., 128
Ethics (Baruch Spinoza), 77
"evolving" Constitution, as opposed to "original intent," 87
eugenics, 160, 161
evidence, direct vs. circumstantial, 125

F

Fifteenth Amendment, 68, 101
"fighting faiths," 133, 166
fires, fascination with, 26, 37, 117–119, 121–122, 127–128, 132–133, 135, 137n., 138, 146, 148, 155
First Amendment, 115–117, 119, 121–122, 127, 128, 132–133, 135, 137n., 138, 140, 146, 148, 155
Fiske, John, 32, 33
Ford, John C., S.J., Father, 62–63
Fourteenth Amendment, 68, 101–102, 105, 108–109, 112, 151, 162
France, 20, 142, 143
Frankfurter, Felix, Justice, 1, 17, 58, 77, 136, 170, 172
Fredericksburg, Battle of, 44
"freedom for the thought that we hate," 115, 155, 166
"freedom of contract," 113
"Freedom of Speech in Wartime," 126–127, 131
Free Speech in the United States, 135
"free trade in ideas," 133, 142
French language, 20
Freund, Ernst, 122ff., 125–126, 137n., 140
Frohwerk v. U.S., 119–120, 131, 132, 137

G

Galsworthy, John, 73
German law, 52, 54
German language, 71, 76
Germany, 119, 127, 129, 132, 141–142, 147
Gettysburg Address, 134–135

INDEX

Gettysburg, Battle of, 40
Ginsburg, Douglas H., 123, 126
Gitlow, Benjamin, 150, 164
Gitlow v. New York, 150, 164–165
governor of South Dakota, 138
Grammar of Assent (John Henry Newman), 74
Greek language, 19, 71, 75, 76
Greek law, 52
Griffith, D.W. (*The Birth of a Nation*), 159
Griswold, Erwin N., 60

H

Hallowell, Norwood Penrose, 34, 43, 47
Hamilton, Alexander, 21
Hand, Learned, Judge, 59n., 77, 123–125, 125n., 167
Harding, President Warren G., 121–122
Harvard College, 24, 25, 30, 31, 34, 35, 37
    A.D. Club, 27, 31
    Hasty Pudding Show, 31
    Memorial Hall, 25
    Porcellian Club, 27, 31
Harvard Law Review, 53, 64
Harvard Law School, 24, 25, 28, 33, 60, 81, 89, 127, 136
Harvard Medical School, 24, 25
Hasty Pudding Show (Harvard College), 31
Hawthorne, Nathaniel, 29, 30, 31

Hazlitt, William, 76
Hegel, Georg Wilhelm Friedrich, 74, 148
Henry IV, 87
Hillenbrand, Laura, 43n.
Hiss, Alger, 1, 17
Hobbes, Thomas, 62, 72–73
Holmes, Abiel (paternal grandfather), 21, 22, 23, 56
    Calvinist minister, 23
Holmes, Amelia (sister), 9, 18, 28, 31
Holmes, Amelia Lee Jackson (mother), 18, 26–27, 41
"Holmesdale" (summer home, 1849–1856, near Pittsfield, Massachusetts), 26–27, 30, 167
Holmes, Edward ("Ned," brother), 18, 28, 31
Holmes, Fanny Dixwell (spouse), 8–9, 14, 22, 32, 33, 34, 37
Holmes, John (uncle), 28
Holmes, Oliver Wendell, Jr., addresses,
    Beverly Farms, Massachusetts, 70, 74, 76, 78–80, 174
    Buzzards Bay, 9, 33
    "Holmesdale" (summer home, 1849–1856, near Pittsfield, Massachusetts), 9, 26–27, 30, 167
    9 Chestnut Street (previously 9 "Orchard"

Street), Beacon Hill,
Boston, 9–10, 11, 92
1720 Eye Street, Washington, D.C., 1, 7–8, 10
10 Beacon Street, Boston, 7, 33, 34
21 Charles Street, Boston, 7, 9, 30
296 Beacon Street, Boston, 7, 10, 32
apologizes, 107, 135
appointed to Massachusetts Supreme Judicial Court, 89
appointed to United States Supreme Court, 95
art, interest in, 71
articles, 64
"a word is not a crystal," 118–119, 166
birthdays, 1, 28, 168, 169, 172
books, interest in, 30, 31, 71–74
fiction, 73–76
CBS radio broadcast, Holmes's farewell speech on, 169
changed mindset, by the Civil War, 37–38, 48
"change of mind," on the First Amendment and free speech, 136ff., 140
Civil War, 26, 32–33, 35, 36, 37ff., 91
"clear and present danger," 117–118, 121, 128, 130, 137n., 152, 166
"combination," in business, 91

"combination in restraint of trade," 95–98
communism, Holmes's skepticism toward, 148, 152
Competition, 91
"counter majoritarian," 156
death of, 172
"Death pluck my ears," 170
deaths witnessed in Civil War, 40, 44
dissents,
Abrams v. U.S., 129ff.
Baltzer v. U.S., 138ff.
Gitlow v. New York, 150ff.
Lochner v. New York, 100ff.
Northern Securities Co. v. U.S., 91–92, 95–99, 107ff.
Plant v. Woods (MSJC), 92–93
Vegelahn v. Guntner (MSJC), 90–91, 92n., 112
U.S. v. Schwimmer, 153–154, 164
education, of a child, 20
elevator, in the homes of, 172
epigrams (see "famous phrases"), 86, 95, 108, 117, 118–119, 133, 150, 165–166
eugenics, progressive attitude toward, 160–161
"falsely shouting fire in a crowded theatre," 26, 117,–118, 166
fame of, 169, 170
family, 18, 20, 21, 26, 31, 90
famous phrases (see "epigrams"), 86, 95, 108,

117, 118–119, 1331, 150, 165–166
fires, fascination with, 26, 37, 117–119, 121–122, 127–128, 132–133, 135, 137n., 138, 146, 148, 155
"free competition," 91
"freedom for the thought that we hate," 115, 155, 166
"free speech," defined, 165
friendship with Louis D. Brandeis, 170–172
gentlemanly language, 83, 85–86
"Great cases, like hard cases, make bad law," 95, 166
great man, Holmes seen as, 170
history of the law, 50, 52
honored as soldier, 46–47
"Hoover Republican," 141
"isms," Holmes's opposition to, 56, 118, 148, 152
jokes, 58, 167, 172
judicial restraint, doctrine of, 99, 101, 107, 110, 111, 111n.
juries, role of, 122–124, 126, 131, 137
labor unions, alleged attitude toward, 90–91, 92–93, 112
languages,
French, 71
German, 71, 76
Greek, 71, 75, 76
Latin, 71, 169
last Supreme Court attendance of, 170

Latin poet, quoting of, 169
letters, 12, 26, 39, 41, 44–45, 58, 61, 66, 72, 75–80, 85, 124, 148, 156, 164, 167
letter to Rosika Schwimmer, 156
"libertarian," 155
library, Justice Holmes's, 70, 72, 73, 77, 80, 172
Lowell Institute lectures, 25, 51, 69, 171
"marketplace of ideas," 134, 166
Marxism, Holmes's skepticism about, 148–149
melancholy, 28
modesty of, 135
monopoly, 92, 95ff.
mother's influence, 26–28
"Natural Law" (article by Holmes, 1918 *Harvard Law Review*), 64, 69
natural rights, 64, 105
nature, love of, 66–67, 166
"opinions that we loathe," 134, 148, 156
"original intent," as opposed to "evolving Constitution," 87
pacifism, Holmes's skepticism toward, 153–155, 164
philosophy, interest in, 51, 57, 62, 64, 71–72, 75, 144, 147
pragmatist, 38, 52, 86
puritanical streak, 21
"questions of fact," in the courtroom, 131, 137

"questions of law," in the courtroom, 131, 137
ranks as a Civil War soldier,
  Captain Holmes, 42, 43, 46, 52
  Lieutenant Colonel Holmes, 38, 45
  Major, 36
reader, 71–77, 80, 166
religious beliefs abandoned, 40, 48, 61–62
resignation from the Union Army, 46
respect for William Howard Taft, 163
retirement, 1, 170–171
"reverse logic," 165–166
Santa Claus, belief in, 172
separate legal rulings from personal views, 112
skepticism, 23, 27, 28, 51, 56–57, 61–62, 66, 118
"skin of a living thought," 119, 166, 167
socialism, Holmes's skepticism towards, 120, 148–150, 152
soldier, 36, 37ff., 47, 89
speeches, 25, 48, 51, 53, 97, 167
speeches on the Civil War, 48
student, 30, 47, 89
"time has upset many fighting faiths . . . ," 133, 166
war, Holmes's attitude toward, 37–40, 48–49, 89, 91
women friends, 33
work, attitude toward, 169
wounds, suffered in the Civil War, 41, 42, 43
writing, 26, 39, 41, 44–45, 58, 61, 66, 71–72, 74–81, 85, 124, 148, 156, 164, 167
wrote mother (Amelia Lee Jackson Holmes), 26, 41
Holmes, Oliver Wendell, Sr., Dr. (father), 5–7, 18, 21, 22–25, 28, 31, 56
  "Breakfast Table" column, 25
  "conceited Dr.," 47
  famous friends and patients, 30, 31
  Harvard connections, 24–25
  Phillips Academy (Andover), heroic punishment at, 5–6, 24
  Paris, studied pathology in, 24, 56
  speech at Memorial Hall, Harvard College, 25
  strained relations with Jr., 27, 35, 44, 46
  youth, 22–23
"Holmes Road" (near Pittsfield, Massachusetts), 30
Homer, 166
Hooker, Joe (Union General), 42
Howe, Julia Ward, 29
Howe, Mark DeWolfe, 28, 80–81
Howells, William Dean, 31
hub of the Hub," 29
"hub of the solar system," 29
Hughes, Charles Evans, Chief Justice, 112

INDEX

Human Nature (Thomas Hobbes), 72
Hume, David, 62
Hurtado v. California, 111

I

ideology, free-market, 107
Illinois law, 102
Illinois Law Review, 140, 145
In Chancery (John Galsworthy), 73
"incitement," 124, 126, 129, 146, 152, 164–165
Irving, Washington, 30

J

Jackson, Charles (maternal grandfather), Judge, 21, 22, 90
James, Henry, 31, 32
James, William, 32
Jefferson, Thomas, 64
Jesuits, 62
Jim Crow segregation, 160
judges as legislators, 103–104
judicial restraint, 99, 101, 107, 110–111, 111n.
judicial review, 102, 123
juries, role of, 122–123, 114, 131, 137
Justice Holmes, Natural Law, and the Supreme Court, 61

K

Kant, Immanuel, 55, 62

Kearsarge Mountain (New Hampshire), 59
Kennedy, Justice Arthur, 84
Keynes, John Maynard, 161
King v. Burwell, 99
Kipling, Rudyard, 35
Ku Klux Klan, 159

L

"laboratory," 19–20, 26, 28, 29
  books, 20, 25–26, 31, 34, 70–77
  family, 18, 20–28, 31, 32, 90
  friends, 20, 29–30, 31–35
  neighborhood, 20, 29–30
  schooling, 20, 30–31
laborers, Justice Holmes supposedly a friend of, 112
labor unions, 90–91, 92–93, 112
laissez-faire, 101, 103, 108, 113
Laski, Harold, 17, 58, 66, 75, 76, 80, 121, 136, 147–149
Leviathan (Thomas Hobbes), 72
Latin language, 19, 44, 169
laudanum, 45
Lenin, Vladimir, 103
Lewis, Anthony, 155
"liberty clause" of the 14th Amendment, 105, 109
liberty of contract, 105, 109
Lincoln, Abraham, 134
"life of the law, the," 50–52, 55, 74, 86
"Lochner Era," 101, 107, 112
"Lochnerizing" a case, 107
Lochner, Joseph, 104–105

Lochner v. New York, 101., 104ff., 109, 110, 111, 112
Lodge, Henry Cabot, 31
Logic (Georg Wilhelm Friedrich Hegel), 74
London, England, 21
Longfellow, Henry Wadsworth, 29, 166
Longfellow family, 30
lotteries, 108
Louisiana, 102
Louisiana statute, 102, 160
Lowell, James Russell, 29, 41
Lowell Lectures, 25, 51, 169, 171
Lucey, Francis E., S.J., 62

M

Macaulay, Thomas, 75
Marx, Karl, 31, 62, 148
Marxism, 148
Massachusetts Supreme Judicial Court, 22, 88–90, 92, 112
Masses Publishing Co. v. Patten, 123–124
measure of Holmes's thought, 164–165
Melville, Herman, 16, 30
Memorial Hall, Harvard College, 25
Mill, James, 19, 22, 26, 31
Mill, John Stuart, 19, 22, 26, 30, 31, 62
Minnesota's rate commission, 102
Moby Dick, 15

"Modern Legal Philosophy Series, The," 147
monopoly, 92, 95ff.
Montaigne, Michel de, 20n., 75
motive of legislature, 106
Muller v. Oregon, 55–56, 159
Munn v. Illinois, 102
Murray, Olivia (Mrs. Bayard Cutting), 59
My Antonia (Willa Cather), 73

N

National Federation of Independent Businesses v. Sebelius, 111
Native Americans, 159
naturalization, 153–159
"natural law," 56–57, 61, 63–64, 68–69, 105
"Natural Law" (article by Holmes, 1918 *Harvard Law Review*), 64, 69
natural rights, 64, 105
"nature," Justice Holmes's love of, 66–67, 166
New Hampshire, 32, 59
Newman, John Henry, Cardinal, 74
New Orleans, 102
New Republic, The, 122, 125–126
Newton, Sir Isaac, 19, 75
New York, city of, 129
New York statute, 105–106, 151, 164
New York statute labor law, 105–106

INDEX

New York Times, The, 160
"Nicodemus house," 43n.
Northern Securities Co. v. U.S., 91–92, 95, 98
Northwestern University Law School, 140
Novick, Sheldon (biographer), 137–138

O

Obergefell v. Hodges, 84
Oklahoma statute, 162
Oliver family, 20
Olney, Richard (Attorney General), 98–99
Olson, Lynne, 135–136, 136n., 161
"original intent," as opposed to "evolving" Constitution, 87
Orley Farm (Anthony Trollope), 74
Ouspensky, Pyotr, 76

P

pacifism, 153–155, 164
"pack the court," 112
Paine, Sumner (cousin, 2nd Lieutenant), 40
Palfrey, John Gorham (executor of Justice Holmes), 174
Park Street Church, basement classroom for T.R. Sullivan's elementary school, 30
"parlor bolsheviks," 143
Pascal, Blaine, 75

"Path of the Law, The" (Jan. 1897), 53–54
Patient Protection and Affordable Care Act (see Affordable Care Act), 99, 103
Peckham, Justice Rufus W., 98, 105, 107
Persae (Aeschylus), 76
Phillips Academy, Andover, 6, 24
Pilgrims, 30
"pink radicals," 143
Pittsfield, Massachusetts, 26–27, 30, 167
Planned Parenthood, 161
Plant v. Woods (Massachusetts Supreme Judicial Court), 92–93
Plessy v. Ferguson, 160
"political offenses," 123
Pollock, Sir Frederick, 17, 77, 80, 145–147
Pollock v. Farmer's Loan & Trust Co., 103
Porcellian Club (Harvard College), 27, 31
Posner, Richard A., Judge, 84, 161
Pound, Roscoe, 55
Princeton University, 160
Progressive Era, 158, 160
progressivism, 158
    alcohol, 158
    antitrust law, 158
    appropriations for roads and bridges, 158
    disfranchisement of black voters, 160

eugenics, 161
immigration restriction laws, 159
Jim Crow segregation, 160
maximum hours, 158
minimum wages, 158
Native Americans, 159
prostitution, 158
racist theories, 158n., 159–161
"reforms," of "others," 146, 160, 161
"separate but equal," 160
Proust, Marcel, 76

Q

Quakers, 34, 155, 165
"questions of fact," 131, 137
"questions of law," 131, 137
question 22 (on Rosika Schwimmer's application for U.S. citizenship), 153
Quincy, Dorothy, 21

R

racist theories, 158n., 159–161
rate-setting, 103–104
Rawls, John, 67–69
Reagan v. Farmer's Loan & Trust Co., 103–104
Reconstruction (or "Civil War") amendments (13th, 14th, 15th), 101
recruiting, obstruction of, 115
"reforms," of "others," 158, 160, 161

Revere, Paul, 41
Roberts, Chief Justice John, 99, 111
Roberts, Justice Owen J., 80, 112, 158
Roman law, 52
Roosevelt, Eleanor, frontispiece, 1
Roosevelt, James (son of Eleanor and Franklin D. Roosevelt), 1
Roosevelt, President Franklin D., frontispiece, 1, 21, 113, 135
Roosevelt, President Theodore, 17, 95, 98, 161
Russell, Bertrand, 65
Russia, 76, 128, 129, 132, 147
Russian Revolution, 117, 148

S

Saint-Beuve, Charles Augustin, 76
Santa Claus, 172
Scalia, Justice Antonin, 83–85, 86
"Scalia's Majoritarian Theocracy" (Richard A. Posner and Eric J. Segall), 84
Schenck v. U.S., 115, 117, 118–119, 120, 131, 132, 137, 138, 152, 154
Schwimmer, Rosika, 114, 153, 156, 164
Scott, Sir Walter, 35
Scottish law, 52
Segall, Eric J., 84
separation-of-powers, principle of, 104, 107
Sermon on the Mount, 155, 166

INDEX

Shaw, George Bernard, 161
Sheehan, Canon Patrick Augustine, 77–79
Sherman Antitrust Law, 79, 91, 95–99
Skinner v. Oklahoma, 162
Slaughterhouse Cases, 102
Smyth v. Ames, 103–104
socialism, 120, 148–149, 152
Socialist Party, 115, 119, 132–133, 150
Socrates, 30, 75
South Dakota, Governor of, 138
speech, crimes committed with, 118
Spencer, Herbert, 62, 101, 108, 166
Spengler, Oswald, 76
Spinoza, Baruch, 77
statute, necessary on sedition, 146
Steele, Richard W., 135
Stephen, Leslie, 54, 167
sterilization, 158, 162
Stevens, Justice John Paul, 109
Stone, Chief Justice Harlan Fiske, 158, 162–163, 170
Stowe, Harriet Beecher, 29, 30
substantive rule of law, 106
Sullivan, T.R. (schoolmaster of Holmes, Jr.), 30
Sullivan's School (elementary school, basement of Park Street Church), 30
Sunday law, 108
Sutherland, Arthur E., 15
Swiss Alps, 167
"switch in time that saved nine," 112

T

Taft, Chief Justice William Howard, 94, 157, 163
Taft Court, 94, 97, 98, 158
tax, federal income, 103, 166n.
Tennyson, Alfred, Lord, 29
Tertium Organum (Pyotr Ouspensky), 76
Thirteenth Amendment, 68, 101
Thoreau, Henry David, 29, 166
Those Angry Days: Roosevelt, Lindbergh, and America's Fight over World War II, 1929–1941 (Lynne Olson), 135–136, 136n.
Thucydides, 75
Ticknor and Fields (publishers), 29
Towne v. Eisner, 119n., 166n.
trial judge, 131, 150, 151
Trollope, Anthony, 74
Trotsky, Leon, 141
Twain, Mark (Samuel Clemens), 29, 35
Twentieth Massachusetts Regiment, 36, 39–40, 43, 46–47

U

United States v. Butler, 79
United States v. Schwimmer, 153, 156, 164–165
Untergang des Abendlanes, Der (Oswald Spengler), 76

Updike, John ("Hub Bids Kid Adieu"), 29
usury laws, 108

V

Vegelahn v. Guntner (Massachusetts Supreme Judicial Court), 90, 93, 11
Virginia statute, 157

W

Walden Pond, 166
Wall Street Journal, 169
Ward, Mrs. Humphrey, 73
Wells, H.G., 161
Wendell family, 20
Wendell, Oliver (great-grandfather), 22
West Coast Hotel v. Parrish, 113
Westminster Review (John Stuart Mill), 20

West Point (United States Military Academy), 161
White, G. Edward (biographer), 156
White, Justice Edward Douglass, 98, 139
Whittier, John Greenleaf, 29
Wigmore, John H., 140–145, 147
Wilde, Oscar, 33
Wilson, President Woodrow, 121–122, 129, 159–161
Wister, Owen, 33
World War I, 115
World War II, 135
Wright, Chauncey, 32
Wu, John C., Dr., 12, 49
Wyzanski, Charles E., 65

Y

Yiddish, 129